United States Laws

Extracts from the Laws of the United States Relating to Currency

and Finance

United States Laws

Extracts from the Laws of the United States Relating to Currency and Finance

ISBN/EAN: 9783744666442

Printed in Europe, USA, Canada, Australia, Japan

Cover: Foto ©Suzi / pixelio.de

More available books at **www.hansebooks.com**

EXTRACTS FROM THE LAWS

OF THE

UNITED STATES

RELATING TO

CURRENCY AND FINANCE.

CAMBRIDGE:

CHARLES W. SEVER,

UNIVERSITY BOOKSTORE.

1885.

UNIVERSITY PRESS:
JOHN WILSON & SON, CAMBRIDGE.

PREFATORY NOTE.

THIS compilation has been made for the purpose of bringing the recent legislation of the United States on the subjects of Currency and Finance within the easy reach of students of political economy. The compiler has selected the leading Acts of Congress which are necessary for an understanding of our financial history since 1860; and has sought, by the omission of such parts as seemed unimportant for the present object and by the condensation of others, to bring into stronger relief the provisions which determine the character of the legislation. Presented thus in their chronological relation, the acts and resolutions of Congress are, it is believed, the best guide in studying the grave economical questions which have come up in the United States during the last fourteen years.

D.

HARVARD COLLEGE, March, 1875.

LEGISLATION

ON

CURRENCY AND FINANCE.

I.... **August, 1846.** — *An Act to provide for the better Organization of the Treasury, and for the Collection, Safe-keeping, Transfer, and Disbursement of the public Revenue.*

Whereas, by the fourth section of the act entitled "An Act to establish the Treasury Department," approved September two, seventeen hundred and eighty-nine, it was provided that it should be the duty of the Treasurer to receive and keep the moneys of the United States, and to disburse the same upon warrants drawn by the Secretary of the Treasury, countersigned by the Comptroller, and recorded by the Register, and not otherwise ; and whereas it is found necessary to make further provisions to enable the Treasurer the better to carry into effect the intent of the said section in relation to the receiving and disbursing the moneys of the United States : Therefore,

Be it enacted by the Senate and House of Representatives of the United States of America in Congress assembled, That the rooms prepared and provided in the new treasury building at the seat of government for the use of the Treasurer of the United States, his assistants and clerks, and occupied by them, and also the fire-proof vaults and safes erected in said rooms for the keeping of the public moneys in the possession and under the immediate control of said Treasurer, and such other apartments as are provided for in this act as places of deposit of the public money, are hereby constituted and declared to be the Treasury of the United States. And all moneys paid into the same shall be subject to the draft of the Treasurer, drawn agreeably to appropriations made by law.

[By sections 2, 3, and 4, and by subsequent acts, the Mint at Philadelphia, and the Branch Mints, the Assay Office at New York, the offices of the Assistant Treasurers at New York, Boston, Philadelphia, Baltimore, Charleston, New Orleans, Cincinnati, Chicago, St. Louis, and San Francisco, and the Depositaries at Buffalo, Pittsburgh, Louisville, Galveston, Santa Fé, and Tucson, are made "places of deposit."]

SEC. 6. *And be it further enacted,* That the Treasurer of the United States, the Treasurer of the Mint of the United States, the treasurers, and those acting as such, of the various branch mints, all collectors of the customs, all surveyors of the customs acting also as collectors, all assistant treasurers, all receivers of public moneys at the several land offices, all postmasters, and all public officers of whatsoever character, be, and they are hereby, required to keep safely, without loaning, using, depositing in banks, or exchanging for other funds than as allowed by this act, all the public money collected by them, or otherwise at any time placed in their possession and custody, till the same is ordered, by the proper department or officer of the government, to be transferred or paid out; and when such orders for transfer or payment are received, faithfully and promptly to make the same as directed. . . .

[Section 9 requires that all collectors and receivers of public moneys shall pay over the same, as often as may be directed by the Secretary of the Treasury or the Postmaster-General, to the Treasurer, assistant treasurer or depositary in their respective cities; and it is made the duty of the Secretary of the Treasury and of the Postmaster-General to direct such payments to be made as often as once in every week.]

SEC. 18. *And be it further enacted,* That on the first day of January, in the year one thousand eight hundred and forty-seven, and thereafter, all duties, taxes, sales of public lands, debts, and sums of money accruing or becoming due to the United States, and also all sums due, for postages or otherwise, to the general post-office department, shall be paid in gold and silver coin only, or in treasury notes issued under the authority of the United States: *Provided,* That the Secretary of the Treasury shall

publish, monthly, in two newspapers at the city of Washington, the amount of specie at the several places of deposit, the amount of treasury notes or drafts issued, and the amount outstanding on the last day of each month.

SEC. 19. *And be it further enacted,* That on the first day of April, one thousand eight hundred and forty-seven, and thereafter, every officer or agent engaged in making disbursements on account of the United States, or of the general post-office, shall make all payments in gold and silver coin, or in treasury notes, if the creditor agree to receive said notes in payment. . . .

[By the Act of March 3, 1857, every officer or agent having money of the United States intrusted to him for disbursement, is required to deposit the same with the Treasurer, or with some Assistant Treasurer or depositary, and to draw for it only in favor of the persons to whom payment is to be made; but money required for payment in sums under twenty dollars can be drawn for by such officer or agent in his own name. 11 Statutes at Large, 249.]

[Approved, August 6, 1846.   9 Statutes at Large, 59.]

II. . . . July, 1861. — *An Act to authorize a National Loan, and for other Purposes.*

Be it enacted, . . . That the Secretary of the Treasury be and he is hereby, authorized to borrow on the credit of the United States, within twelve months from the passage of this act, a sum not exceeding two hundred and fifty millions of dollars, or so much thereof as he may deem necessary for the public service, for which he is authorized to issue coupon bonds, or registered bonds, or treasury notes, in such proportions of each as he may deem advisable; the bonds to bear interest not exceeding seven per centum per annum, payable semi-annually, irredeemable for twenty years, and after that period redeemable at the pleasure of the United States; and the treasury notes to be of any denomination fixed by the Secretary of the Treasury, not less than fifty dollars, and to be payable three years after date, with interest at the rate of seven and three tenths per centum per annum, payable semi-annually.   And the Secretary of the Treasury may also issue in exchange for coin, and as part of the above loan, or may pay for salaries or other dues from the United States, treasury

notes of a less denomination than fifty dollars, not bearing interest, but payable on demand by the Assistant Treasurers of the
United States at Philadelphia, New York, or Boston, or treasury notes bearing interest at the rate of three and sixty-five
hundredths per centum, payable in one year from date, and exchangeable at any time for treasury notes for fifty dollars, and
upwards, issuable under the authority of this act, and bearing
interest as specified above : *Provided*, That no exchange of such
notes in any less amount than one hundred dollars shall be made
at any one time : *And provided further*, That no treasury notes
shall be issued of a less denomination than ten dollars, and that
the whole amount of treasury notes, not bearing interest, issued
under the authority of this act, shall not exceed fifty millions of
dollars.

[Section 3 authorizes the Secretary of the Treasury to open books for
subscriptions for the treasury notes, at such places as he may select; and,
if he thinks expedient, before opening such books, to pay out for public
dues, or for coin, or for the public debt, any amount of said treasury
notes not exceeding one hundred millions of dollars.

Section 4 provides for the issue of proposals in the United States for
such portion of the loan in bonds as the Secretary may determine, "*Provided*, That no offer shall be accepted at less than par."

Section 5 authorizes the Secretary of the Treasury to negotiate any
part of the loan, not exceeding one hundred millions of dollars, in any
foreign country; to make the principal and interest payable either in
the United States or in Europe; and to fix the rate of exchange at which
the principal shall be received, which rate shall also be the rate of exchange for the payment of the principal and interest in Europe.]

SEC. 6. *And be it further enacted*, That whenever any treasury notes of a denomination less than fifty dollars, authorized to
be issued by this act, shall have been redeemed, the Secretary
of the Treasury may reissue the same, or may cancel them and
issue new notes to an equal amount: *Provided*, That the aggregate amounts of bonds and treasury notes issued under the
foregoing provisions of this act shall never exceed the full
amount authorized by the first section of this act; and the power
to issue or reissue such notes shall cease and determine after the
thirty-first of December, eighteen hundred and sixty-two.

SEC. 7. *And be it further enacted*, That the Secretary of the
Treasury is hereby authorized, whenever he shall deem it expe-

dient, to issue in exchange for coin, or in payment for publi
dues, treasury notes of any of the denominations hereinbefor
specified, bearing interest not exceeding six per centum per annum
and payable at any time not exceeding twelve months from date
provided that the amount of notes so issued, or paid, shall at no
time exceed twenty millions of dollars.

[Approved, July 17, 1861.   12 Statutes at Large, 259.

III. ... August, 1861. — *An Act supplementary to an Act entitle*
"An Act to authorize a National Loan, and for other Pur
poses."

[Section 1 authorizes the Secretary of the Treasury to issue bond
bearing interest at six per cent. per annum, and payable at the pleasur
of the United States after twenty years from date, to be given in ex
change for such treasury notes, bearing interest at seven and three-tenth
per cent., issued under the act of July 17, 1861, as the holders may presen
for exchange before or at the maturity thereof. Any part of the treasur;
notes payable on demand, authorized by said act, may be made payabl
by the Assistant Treasurer at St. Louis, or the depositary at Cincinnati.

SEC. 3. *And be it further enacted,* That so much of the ac
to which this is supplementary as limits the denomination of ;
portion of the treasury notes authorized by said act at not les
than ten dollars, be and is so modified as to authorize the Sec
retary of the Treasury to fix the denomination of said notes a
not less than five dollars.

SEC. 5. *And be it further enacted,* That the treasury note;
authorized by the act to which this is supplementary, of a les;
denomination than fifty dollars, payable on demand without in
terest, and not exceeding in amount the sum of fifty millions of
dollars, shall be receivable in payment of public dues.

SEC. 6. *And be it further enacted,* That the provisions of the
act entitled "An act to provide for the better organization of
the Treasury, and for the collection, safe-keeping, transfer
and disbursements of the public revenue," passed August six
eighteen hundred and forty-six, be and the same are hereby
suspended, so far as to allow the Secretary of the Treasury to
deposit any of the moneys obtained on any of the loans now
authorized by law, to the credit of the Treasurer of the United
States, in such solvent specie-paying banks as he may select;

and the said moneys, so deposited, may be withdrawn from such
deposit for deposit with the regular authorized depositaries, or
for the payment of public dues, or paid in redemption of the
notes authorized to be issued under this act, or the act to which
this is supplementary, payable on demand, as may seem expedient
to, or be directed by, the Secretary of the Treasury.

SEC. 7. *And be it further enacted,* That the Secretary of the
Treasury may sell or negotiate, for any portion of the loan provided for in the act to which this is supplementary, bonds payable not more than twenty years from date, and bearing interest
not exceeding six per centum per annum, payable semi-annually,
at any rate not less than the equivalent of par, for the bonds
bearing seven per centum interest, authorized by said act.

[Approved, August 5, 1861.   12 Statutes at Large, 313.]

IV.... February, 1862.—*An Act to authorize an additional Issue of United States Notes.*

Be it enacted, . . . That the Secretary of the Treasury, in
addition to the fifty millions of notes payable on demand of denominations not less than five dollars, heretofore authorized by
the acts of July seventeenth and August fifth, eighteen hundred
and sixty-one, be, and he is hereby, authorized to issue like
notes, and for like purposes, to the amount of ten millions of
dollars, and said notes shall be deemed part of the loan of two
hundred and fifty millions of dollars authorized by said acts.

[Approved, February 12, 1862.   12 Statutes at Large, 338.]

V..., February, 1862. — *An Act to authorize the Issue of United States Notes, and for the Redemption or Funding thereof, and for Funding the Floating Debt of the United States.*

Be it enacted, . . . That the Secretary of the Treasury is
hereby authorized to issue, on the credit of the United States, one
hundred and fifty millions of dollars of United States notes, not
bearing interest, payable to bearer, at the Treasury of the United
States, and of such denominations as he may deem expedient,
not less than five dollars each: *Provided, however,* That fifty
millions of said notes shall be in lieu of the demand treasury

notes authorized to be issued by the act of July seventeen, eighteen hundred and sixty-one; which said demand notes shall be taken up as rapidly as practicable, and the notes herein provided for substituted for them: *And provided further*, That the amount of the two kinds of notes together shall at no time exceed the sum of one hundred and fifty millions of dollars, and such notes herein authorized shall be receivable in payment of all taxes, internal duties, excises, debts, and demands of every kind due to the United States, except duties on imports, and of all claims and demands against the United States of every kind whatsoever, except for interest upon bonds and notes, which shall be paid in coin, and shall also be lawful money and a legal tender in payment of all debts, public and private, within the United States, except duties on imports and interest as aforesaid. And any holders of said United States notes depositing any sum not less than fifty dollars, or some multiple of fifty dollars, with the Treasurer of the United States, or either of the Assistant Treasurers, shall receive in exchange therefor duplicate certificates of deposit, one of which may be transmitted to the Secretary of the Treasury, who shall thereupon issue to the holder an equal amount of bonds of the United States, coupon or registered, as may by said holder be desired, bearing interest at the rate of six per centum per annum, payable semi-annually, and redeemable at the pleasure of the United States after five years, and payable twenty years from the date thereof. And such United States notes shall be received the same as coin, at their par value, in payment for any loans that may be hereafter sold or negotiated by the Secretary of the Treasury, and may be re-issued from time to time as the exigencies of the public interests shall require.

SEC. 2. *And be it further enacted*, That to enable the Secretary of the Treasury to fund the treasury notes and floating debt of the United States, he is hereby authorized to issue, on the credit of the United States, coupon bonds, or registered bonds, to an amount not exceeding five hundred millions of dollars, redeemable at the pleasure of the United States after five years, and payable twenty years from date, and bearing interest at the rate of six per centum per annum, payable semi-annually. And the bonds herein authorized shall be of such denominations, not less than fifty dollars, as may be determined upon by the Secretary of the Treasury. And the Secretary of the Treasury may dispose of such bonds at any time, at the market value thereof, for the coin of the United States, or for any of the treasury notes that have been or may hereafter be issued under any former act of Congress, or for United States notes that may be issued under the provisions of this act; and all stocks, bonds, and other securities of the United States held by individuals, corporations, or .associations, within the United States, shall be exempt from taxation by or under State authority.

SEC. 4. *And be it further enacted,* That the Secretary of the Treasury may receive from any person or persons, or any corporation, United States notes on deposit for not less than thirty days, in sums of not less than one hundred dollars, with any of the Assistant Treasurers or designated depositaries of the United States authorized by the Secretary of the Treasury to receive them, who shall issue therefor certificates of deposit, made in such form as the Secretary of the Treasury shall prescribe, and said certificates of deposit shall bear interest at the rate of five per centum per annum; and any amount of United States notes so deposited may be withdrawn from deposit at any time after ten days' notice on the return of said certificates: *Provided,* That the interest on all such deposits shall cease and determine at the pleasure of the Secretary of the Treasury: *And provided further,* That the aggregate of such deposit shall at no time exceed the amount of twenty-five millions of dollars.

SEC. 5. *And be it further enacted,* That all duties on imported goods shall be paid in coin, or in notes payable on demand heretofore authorized to be issued and by law receivable in payment of public dues, and the coin so paid shall be set apart as a special fund, and shall be applied as follows:

First. To the payment in coin of the interest on the bonds and notes of the United States.

Second. To the purchase or payment of one per centum of the entire debt of the United States, to be made within each fiscal year after the first day of July, eighteen hundred and sixty-two, which is to be set apart as a sinking fund, and the interest of which shall in like manner be applied to the purchase or pay

ment of the public debt as the Secretary of the Treasury shall from time to time direct.

Third. The residue thereof to be paid into the Treasury of the United States.

[Approved, February 25, 1862. 12 Statutes at Large, 345.]

VI ... March, 1862. — *An Act to authorize the Secretary of the Treasury to issue Certificates of Indebtedness to Public Creditors.*

Be it enacted, . . . That the Secretary of the Treasury be, and he is hereby authorized, to cause to be issued to any public creditor who may be desirous to receive the same, upon requisition of the head of the proper department in satisfaction of audited and settled demands against the United States, certificates for the whole amount due or parts thereof not less than one thousand dollars, signed by the Treasurer of the United States, and countersigned as may be directed by the Secretary of the Treasury; which certificates shall be payable in one year from date or earlier, at the option of the Government, and shall bear interest at the rate of six per centum per annum.

[Approved, March 1, 1862. 12 Statutes at Large, 352.]

VII ... March, 1862. — *An Act to authorize the Purchase of Coin, and for other Purposes.*

Be it enacted, . . . That the Secretary of the Treasury may purchase coin with any of the bonds or notes of the United States, authorized by law, at such rates and upon such terms as he may deem most advantageous to the public interest; and may issue, under such rules and regulations as he may prescribe, certificates of indebtedness, such as are authorized by an act entitled " An act to authorize the Secretary of the Treasury to issue certificates of indebtedness to public creditors," approved March first, eighteen hundred and sixty-two, to such creditors as may desire to receive the same, in discharge of checks drawn by disbursing officers upon sums placed to their credit on the books of the Treasurer, upon requisitions of the proper departments, as well as in discharge of audited and settled accounts, as provided by said act.

SEC. 2. *And be it further enacted*, That the demand-notes
authorized by the act of July seventeenth, eighteen hundred and
sixty-one, and by the act of February twelfth, eighteen hundred
and sixty-two, shall, in addition to being receivable in payment
of duties on imports, be receivable, and shall be lawful money
and a legal tender, in like manner, and for the same purposes,
and to the same extent, as the notes authorized by an act entitled " An act to authorize the issue of United States notes,
and for the redemption or funding thereof, and for funding the
floating debt of the United States," approved February twenty-
fifth, eighteen hundred and sixty-two.

SEC. 3. *And be it further enacted*, That the limitation upon
temporary deposits of United States notes with any Assistant
Treasurers or designated depositaries, authorized by the Secretary of the Treasury to receive such deposits, at five per cent.
interest, to twenty-five millions of dollars, shall be so far modified as to authorize the Secretary of the Treasury to receive
such deposits to an amount not exceeding fifty millions of dollars,
and that the rates of interest shall be prescribed by the Secretary of the Treasury not exceeding the annual rate of five per
centum.

[Approved, March 17, 1862.   12 Statutes at Large, 370.]

VIII ... July, 1862. — *An Act to authorize an additional Issue
of United States Notes, and for other Purposes.*

Be it enacted, . . . That the Secretary of the Treasury
is hereby authorized to issue, in addition to the amounts heretofore authorized, on the credit of the United States, one hundred
and fifty millions of dollars of United States notes, not bearing
interest, payable to bearer at the Treasury of the United States,
and of such denominations as he may deem expedient: *Provided*,
That no note shall be issued for the fractional part of a dollar,
and not more than thirty-five millions shall be of lower denominations than five dollars; and such notes shall be receivable
in payment of all loans made to the United States, and of all
taxes, internal duties, excises, debts, and demands of every kind
due to the United States, except duties on imports and interest,

and of all claims and demands against the United States, except
for interest upon bonds, notes, and certificates of debt or deposit;
and shall also be lawful money and a legal tender in payment of
all debts, public and private, within the United States, except
duties on imports and interest, as aforesaid.   And any holder of
said United States notes depositing any sum not less than fifty
dollars, or some multiple of fifty dollars, with the Treasurer of
the United States, or either of the assistant treasurers, shall receive in exchange therefor duplicate certificates of deposit, one
of which may be transmitted to the Secretary of the Treasury,
who shall thereupon issue to the holder an equal amount of bonds
of the United States, coupon or registered, as may by said holder
be desired, bearing interest at the rate of six per centum per annum, payable semi-annually, and redeemable at the pleasure of
the United States after five years, and payable twenty years
from the date thereof: *Provided, however,* That any notes issued
under this act may be paid in coin, instead of being received in
exchange for certificates of deposit as above specified, at the
direction of the Secretary of the Treasury. And the Secretary
of the Treasury may exchange for such notes, on such terms as
he shall think most beneficial to the public interest, any bonds of
the United States bearing six per centum interest, and redeemable after five and payable in twenty years, which have been or
may be lawfully issued under the provisions of any existing act;
may reissue the notes so received in exchange; may receive
and cancel any notes heretofore lawfully issued under any act of
Congress, and in lieu thereof issue an equal amount in notes
such as are authorized by this act; and may purchase, at rates
not exceeding that of the current market, and cost of purchase not
exceeding one-eighth of one per centum, any bonds or certificates of debt of the United States as he may deem advisable.

SEC. 3. *And be it further enacted,* That the limitation upon
temporary deposits of United States notes with any Assistant
Treasurer or designated depositary authorized by the Secretary
of the Treasury to receive such deposits, to fifty millions of dollars be, and is hereby, repealed; and the Secretary of the Treasury is authorized to receive such deposits, under such regulations
as he may prescribe, to such amount as he may deem expedient,

not exceeding one hundred millions of dollars, for not less than thirty days, in sums not less than one hundred dollars, at a rate of interest not exceeding five per centum per annum; and any amount so deposited may be withdrawn from deposit, at any time after ten days' notice, on the return of the certificate of deposit. And of the amount of United States notes authorized by this act, not less than fifty millions of dollars shall be reserved for the purpose of securing prompt payment of such deposits when demanded, and shall be issued and used only when, in the judgment of the Secretary of the Treasury, the same or any part thereof may be needed for that purpose. And certificates of deposit and of indebtedness issued under this or former acts may be received on the same terms as United States notes in payment for bonds redeemable after five and payable in twenty years.

SEC. 4. *And be it further enacted,* That the Secretary of the Treasury may, at any time until otherwise ordered by Congress, and under the restrictions imposed by the " Act to authorize a national loan, and for other purposes," borrow, on the credit of the United States, such part of the sum of two hundred and fifty millions mentioned in said act as may not have been borrowed, under the provisions of the same, within twelve months from the passage thereof.

SEC. 6. *And be it further enacted,* That all the provisions of the act entitled " An act to authorize the issue of United States notes, and for the redemption or funding thereof, and for funding the floating debt of the United States," approved February twenty-five, eighteen hundred and sixty-two, so far as the same can or may be applied to the provisions of this act, and not inconsistent therewith, shall apply to the notes hereby authorized to be issued.

[Approved, July 11, 1862. 12 Statutes at Large, p. 532.]

IX....July, 1862. — *An Act to authorize Payments in Stamps, and to prohibit Circulation of Notes of less Denomination than One Dollar.*

Be it enacted, . . . That the Secretary of the Treasury be, and he is hereby directed to furnish to the Assistant Treasurers, and such designated depositaries of the United States as

may be by him selected, in such sums as he may deem expedient, the postage and other stamps of the United States, to be exchanged by them, on application, for United States notes; and from and after the first day of August next such stamps shall be receivable in payment of all dues to the United States less than five dollars, and shall be received in exchange for United States notes when presented to any Assistant Treasurer or any designated depositary selected as aforesaid in sums not less than five dollars.

SEC. 2. *And be it further enacted,* That from and after the first day of August, eighteen hundred and sixty-two, no private corporation, banking association, firm, or individual shall make, issue, circulate, or pay any note, check, memorandum, token, or other obligation, for a less sum than one dollar, intended to circulate as money or to be received or used in lieu of lawful money of the United States. . . .

[Approved, July 17, 1862.   12 Statutes at Large, 592.]

X. . . . January, 1863. — *Joint Resolution to provide for the immediate Payment of the Army and Navy of the United States.*

Whereas it is deemed expedient to make immediate provision for the payment of the army and navy : therefore,

Be it resolved, . . . That the Secretary of the Treasury be, and he is hereby, authorized, if required by the exigencies of the public service, to issue on the credit of the United States the sum of one hundred millions of dollars of United States notes, in such form as he may deem expedient, not bearing interest, payable to bearer on demand, and of such denominations not less than one dollar, as he may prescribe, which notes so issued shall be lawful money and a legal tender, like the similar notes heretofore authorized in payment of all debts, public and private, within the United States, except for duties on imports and interest on the public debt ; and the notes so issued shall be part of the amount provided for in any bill now pending for the issue of treasury notes, or that may be passed hereafter by this Congress.

[Approved, January 17, 1863.   12 Statutes at Large, p. 822.]

2

XI.... February, 1863. — *An Act to provide a National Currency, secured by a Pledge of United States Stocks, and to provide for the Circulation and Redemption thereof.*

[This act was repealed and superseded by the act of similar title approved June 3, 1864. For the principal points of difference between the two acts, see the note on p. 34.]

[Approved, February 25, 1863. 12 Statutes at Large, 665.]

XII.... March, 1863. — *An Act to provide Ways and Means for the Support of the Government.*

Be it enacted, . . . That the Secretary of the Treasury be, and he is hereby, authorized to borrow, from time to time, on the credit of the United States, a sum not exceeding three hundred millions of dollars for the current fiscal year, and six hundred millions for the next fiscal year, and to issue therefor coupon or registered bonds, payable at the pleasure of the government after such periods as may be fixed by the Secretary, not less than ten nor more than forty years from date, in coin, and of such denominations not less than fifty dollars, as he may deem expedient, bearing interest at a rate not exceeding six per centum per annum, payable on bonds not exceeding one hundred dollars, annually, and on all other bonds semi-annually, in coin; and he may in his discretion dispose of such bonds at any time, upon such terms as he may deem most advisable, for lawful money of the United States, or for any of the certificates of indebtedness or deposit that may at any time be unpaid, or for any of the treasury notes heretofore issued or which may be issued under the provisions of this act. And all the bonds and treasury notes or United States notes issued under the provisions of this act shall be exempt from taxation by or under State or municipal authority: *Provided,* That there shall be outstanding of bonds, treasury notes, and United States notes, at any time, issued under the provisions of this act, no greater amount altogether than the sum of nine hundred millions of dollars.

SEC. 2. *And be it further enacted,* That the Secretary of the Treasury be, and he is hereby, authorized to issue, on the credit of the United States, four hundred millions of dollars in treasury notes, payable at the pleasure of the United States, or at

.

[handwritten marginal notes: Post-note 400 m. of three. notes to run not over 3 yrs. with not over 6 4/0]

such time or times not exceeding three years from date, as may be found most beneficial to the public interest, and bearing interest at a rate not exceeding six per centum per annum, payable at periods expressed on the face of said treasury notes; and the interest on the said treasury notes and on certificates of indebtedness and deposit hereafter issued, shall be paid in lawful money. The treasury notes thus issued shall be of such denomination as the Secretary may direct, not less than ten dollars, and may be disposed of on the best terms that can be obtained, or may be paid to any creditor of the United States willing to receive the same at par. And said treasury notes may be made a legal tender to the same extent as United States notes, for their face value excluding interest; or they may be made exchangeable under regulations prescribed by the Secretary of the Treasury, by the holder thereof, at the Treasury in the city of Washington, or at the office of any Assistant Treasurer or depositary designated for that purpose, for United States notes equal in amount to the treasury notes offered for exchange, together with the interest accrued and due thereon at the date of interest payment next preceding such exchange. And in lieu of any amount of said treasury notes thus exchanged, or redeemed or paid at maturity, the Secretary may issue an equal amount of other treasury notes; and the treasury notes so exchanged, redeemed, or paid, shall be cancelled and destroyed as the Secretary may direct. In order to secure certain and prompt exchanges of United States notes for treasury notes, when required as above provided, the Secretary shall have power to issue United States notes to the amount of one hundred and fifty millions of dollars, which may be used if necessary for such exchanges; but no part of the United States notes authorized by this section shall be issued for or applied to any other purposes than said exchanges; and whenever any amount shall have been so issued and applied, the same shall be replaced as soon as practicable from the sales of treasury notes for United States notes.

[handwritten marginal notes: to be greater than 10: to be legal tender for face value. / Re-issue.]

SEC. 3. *And be it further enacted,* That the Secretary of the Treasury be, and he is hereby, authorized, if required by the exigencies of the public service, for the payment of the army and navy, and other creditors of the government, to issue on the credit of the United States the sum of one hundred and fifty millions of dollars of United States notes, including the amount of such notes heretofore authorized by the joint resolution approved January seventeen, eighteen hundred and sixty-three, in such form as he may deem expedient, not bearing interest, payable to bearer, and of such denominations, not less than one dollar, as he may prescribe, which notes so issued shall be lawful money and a legal tender in payment of all debts, public and private, within the United States, except for duties on imports and interest on the public debt; and any of the said notes, when returned to the Treasury, may be re-issued from time to time as the exigencies of the public service may require. And in lieu of any of said notes, or any other United States notes, returned to the Treasury, and cancelled or destroyed, there may be issued equal amounts of United States notes, such as are authorized by this act. And so much of the act to authorize the issue of United States notes, and for other purposes, approved February twenty-five, eighteen hundred and sixty-two, and of the act to authorize an additional issue of United States notes, and for other purposes, approved July eleven, eighteen hundred and sixty-two, as restricts the negotiation of bonds to market value, is hereby repealed. And the holders of United States notes, issued under and by virtue of said acts, shall present the same for the purpose of exchanging the same for bonds, as therein provided, on or before the first day of July, eighteen hundred and sixty-three, and thereafter the right so to exchange the same shall cease and determine.

SEC. 4. *And be it further enacted,* That in lieu of postage and revenue stamps for fractional currency, and of fractional notes, commonly called postage currency, issued or to be issued, the Secretary of the Treasury may issue fractional notes of like amounts in such form as he may deem expedient, and may provide for the engraving, preparation and issue thereof, in the Treasury Department building. And all such notes issued shall be exchangeable by the Assistant Treasurers and designated depositaries for United States notes, in sums not less than three dollars, and shall be receivable for postage and revenue stamps, and also in payment of any dues to the United States less than

five dollars, except duties on imports, and shall be redeemed on presentation at the Treasury of the United States in such sums and under such regulations as the Secretary of the Treasury shall prescribe : *Provided,* That the whole amount of fractional currency issued, including postage and revenue stamps issued as currency, shall not exceed fifty millions of dollars.

SEC. 5. *And be it further enacted,* That the Secretary of the Treasury is hereby authorized to receive deposits of gold coin and bullion with the Treasurer or any Assistant Treasurer of the United States, in sums not less than twenty dollars, and to issue certificates therefor, in denominations of not less than twenty dollars each, corresponding with the denominations of the United States notes. The coin and bullion deposited for or representing the certificates of deposit shall be retained in the Treasury for the payment of the same on demand. And certificates representing coin in the Treasury may be issued in payment of interest on the public debt, which certificates, together with those issued for coin and bullion deposited, shall not at any time exceed twenty per centum beyond the amount of coin and bullion in the Treasury; and the certificates for coin or bullion in the Treasury shall be received at par in payment for duties on imports.

[Section 7, after providing for taxes to be laid upon the circulation of all banks and corporations, whether established under state laws or under the act of February 25, 1863, directs that all banks, corporations, or individuals issuing notes for any fractional part of a dollar after April 1, 1863, shall be taxed ten per cent. per annum upon the amount of such fractional notes.]

[Approved, March 3, 1863.   12 Statutes at Large, 709.]

XIII.... March, 1864. — *An Act supplementary to an Act entitled* " *An Act to provide Ways and Means for the Support of the Government,*" *approved March third, eighteen hundred and sixty-three.*

[Section 1 provides that in lieu of so much of the loan authorized by the Act of March 3, 1863, the Secretary of the Treasury may issue not exceeding two hundred millions of dollars of coupon or registered bonds, redeemable not less than five years and payable not more than forty years from date in coin, with the same provisions as to denomination, interest, method of disposal, and exemption from taxation as in section 1 of the Act of March 3, 1863.

Section 2 authorizes the Secretary of the Treasury to issue bonds under the Act of February 25, 1862, in excess of five hundred millions of dollars, to the amount of eleven millions, to such persons as subscribed for them on or before January 21, 1864, and have paid for them.]

[Approved, March 3, 1864.   13 Statutes at Large, 13]

XIV.... March, 1864. — *Joint Resolution to authorize the Secretary of the Treasury to anticipate the Payment of Interest on the Public Debt, and for other Purposes.*

Be it resolved, . . . That the Secretary of the Treasury be authorized to anticipate the payment of interest on the public debt, by a period not exceeding one year, from time to time, either with or without a rebate of interest upon the coupons, as to him may seem expedient; and he is hereby authorized to dispose of any gold in the Treasury of the United States not necessary for the payment of interest of the public debt: *Provided,* That the obligation to create the sinking fund according to the Act of February twenty-fifth, eighteen hundred and sixty-two, shall not be impaired thereby.

[Approved, March 17, 1864.   13 Statutes at Large, 404.]

XV.... June, 1864. — *An Act to provide a National Currency, secured by a Pledge of United States Bonds, and to provide for the Circulation and Redemption thereof.*

Be it enacted, . . . That there shall be established in the Treasury Department a separate bureau, which shall be charged with the execution of this and all other laws that may be passed by Congress respecting the issue and regulation of a national currency secured by United States bonds.   The chief officer of the said bureau shall be denominated the Comptroller of the Currency, and shall be under the general direction of the Secretary of the Treasury.   He shall be appointed by the President, on the recommendation of the Secretary of the Treasury, by and with the advice and consent of the Senate, and shall hold his office for the term of five years unless sooner removed by the President, upon reasons to be communicated by him to the Senate; he shall receive an annual salary of five thousand dollars. . . .

[He shall give a bond in the penalty of $100,000 for the faithful discharge of his duties; shall have a competent deputy, who shall give a

like bond for $50,000; and neither the Comptroller nor the Deputy-Comptroller shall "be interested" in any association issuing currency under the provisions of this act.

Section 5 provides that an association for carrying on the business of banking may be formed by any number of persons not less than five, who shall enter into articles stating the object of the association and containing provisions for regulating its business not inconsistent with this act. A copy of these articles must be forwarded to the Comptroller, together with a certificate of organization, specifying the name of the association, which shall be subject to the approval of the Comptroller, the place where it is located, the amount of its capital, and the names and residences of its stockholders. But the association shall not begin the business of banking until it is authorized by the Comptroller. It shall be a body-corporate from the date of its organization-certificate, and shall continue for twenty years unless sooner dissolved under the provisions of this act, and shall have all such incidental powers as are necessary to carry on the business of banking, by discounting, receiving deposits, lending money on personal security, buying and selling exchange, coin and bullion, and issuing and circulating notes under the provisions of this act.]

SEC. 7. *And be it further enacted,* That no association shall be organized under this act, with a less capital than one hundred thousand dollars, nor in a city whose population exceeds fifty thousand persons, with a less capital than two hundred thousand dollars: *Provided,* That banks with a capital of not less than fifty thousand dollars may, with the approval of the Secretary of the Treasury, be organized in any place the population of which does not exceed six thousand inhabitants.

[Every association is to be managed by not less than five directors, one of whom shall be its president; every director must own at least ten shares of the capital stock in his own right and in no way pledged for any debt; all elections of directors, after the first, are to be held annually in the month of January; every shareholder is to have one vote for every share of the stock owned by him; but no shareholder whose liability is past due and unpaid is to be allowed to vote.]

SEC. 12. *And be it further enacted,* That the capital stock of any association formed under this act shall be divided into shares of one hundred dollars each, and be deemed personal property and transferable on the books of the association in such manner as may be prescribed in the by-laws or articles of association. . . . The shareholders of each association formed under the provisions of this act, and of each existing bank or banking asso-

ciation that may accept the provisions of this act, shall be held
individually responsible, equally and ratably, and not one for
another, for all contracts, debts, and engagements of such association to the extent of the amount of their stock therein at the
par value thereof, in addition to the amount invested in such
shares. . . .

[But shareholders of any banking association now existing under
State laws, having not less than five millions of capital and a surplus of
twenty per cent. on hand, shall be liable only to the amount invested in
their shares ; but said surplus shall be in addition to that elsewhere required by this act, and shall be kept undiminished.

Section 13 provides that any association may increase its capital or
may diminish the same, subject to the approval of the Comptroller.]

SEC. 14. *And be it further enacted,* That at least fifty per
centum of the capital stock of every association shall be paid in
before it shall be authorized to commence business ; and the remainder of the capital stock of such association shall be paid in
instalments of at least ten per centum each on the whole amount
of the capital as frequently as one instalment at the end of each
succeeding month from the time it shall be authorized by the
Comptroller to commence business ; and the payment of each
instalment shall be certified to the Comptroller, under oath, by
the president or cashier of the association.

SEC. 16. *And be it further enacted,* That every association,
after having complied with the provisions of this act, preliminary
to the commencement of banking business under its provisions,
and before it shall be authorized to commence business, shall transfer and deliver to the Treasurer of the United States any United
States registered bonds bearing interest to an amount not less
than thirty thousand dollars nor less than one third of the capital
stock paid in, which bonds shall be deposited with the Treasurer
of the United States and by him safely kept in his office until the
same shall be otherwise disposed of, in pursuance of the provisions of this act. . . . And the deposit of bonds shall be, by every
association, increased as its capital may be paid up or increased, so
that every association shall at all times have on deposit with the
Treasurer registered United States bonds to the amount of at
least one third of its capital stock actually paid in : *Provided,*

That nothing in this section shall prevent an association that may desire to reduce its capital or to close up its business and dissolve its organization from taking up its bonds upon returning to the Comptroller its circulating notes in the proportion hereinafter named in this act, nor from taking up any excess of bonds beyond one third of its capital stock and upon which no circulating notes have been delivered.

SEC. 21. *And be it further enacted,* That upon the transfer and delivery of bonds to the Treasurer, as provided in the foregoing section, the association making the same shall be entitled to receive from the Comptroller of the Currency circulating notes of different denominations, in blank, registered and countersigned as hereinafter provided, equal in amount to ninety per centum of the current market value of the United States bonds so transferred and delivered, but not exceeding ninety per centum of the amount of said bonds at the par value thereof, if bearing interest at a rate not less than five per centum per annum ; and at no time shall the total amount of such notes, issued to any such association, exceed the amount at such time actually paid in of its capital stock.

SEC. 22. *And be it further enacted,* That the entire amount of notes for circulation to be issued under this act shall not exceed three hundred millions of dollars. In order to furnish suitable notes for circulation, the Comptroller of the Currency is hereby authorized and required, under the direction of the Secretary of the Treasury, to cause plates and dies to be engraved, in the best manner to guard against counterfeiting and fraudulent alterations, and to have printed therefrom, and numbered, such quantity of circulating notes, in blank, of the denominations of one dollar, two dollars, three dollars, five dollars, ten dollars, twenty dollars, fifty dollars, one hundred dollars, five hundred dollars, and one thousand dollars, as may be required to supply, under this act, the associations entitled to receive the same ; which notes shall express upon their face that they are secured by United States bonds, deposited with the Treasurer of the United States by the written or engraved signatures of the Treasurer and Register, and by the imprint of the seal of the Treasury ; and shall also express upon their face the promise of the association receiving the same to pay on demand, attested by the signatures of the president or vice-president and cashier. And the said notes shall bear such devices and such other statements, and shall be in such form, as the Secretary of the Treasury shall, by regulation, direct : *Provided*, That not more than one-sixth part of the notes furnished to an association shall be of a less denomination than five dollars, and that after specie payments shall be resumed no association shall be furnished with notes of a less denomination than five dollars.

SEC. 23. *And be it further enacted*, That after any such association shall have caused its promise to pay such notes on demand to be signed by the president or vice-president and cashier thereof, in such manner as to make them obligatory promissory notes, payable on demand, at its place of business, such association is hereby authorized to issue and circulate the same as money ; and the same shall be received at par in all parts of the United States in payment of taxes, excises, public lands, and all other dues to the United States, except for duties on imports ; and also for all salaries and other debts and demands owing by the United States to individuals, corporations, and associations within the United States, except interest on the public debt, and in redemption of the national currency. And no such association shall issue post notes or any other notes to circulate as money than such as are authorized by the foregoing provisions of this act.

[Section 24 provides that the Comptroller shall receive the worn-out or mutilated notes of any association, and shall deliver to it fresh notes in place thereof, and that the worn-out or mutilated notes shall be burned in presence of four persons, appointed by the Secretary of the Treasury, the Comptroller, the Treasurer of the United States and the association, respectively.]

SEC. 26. *And be it further enacted*, That the bonds transferred to and deposited with the Treasurer of the United States, as hereinbefore provided, by any banking association for the security of its circulating notes, shall be held exclusively for that purpose, until such notes shall be redeemed, except as provided in this act ; but the Comptroller of the Currency shall give to

any such banking association powers of attorney to receive and appropriate to its own use the interest on the bonds which it shall have so transferred to the Treasurer; but such powers shall become inoperative whenever such banking association shall fail to redeem its circulating notes as aforesaid. Whenever the market or cash value of any bonds deposited with the Treasurer of the United States, as aforesaid, shall be reduced below the amount of the circulation issued for the same, the Comptroller of the Currency is hereby authorized to demand and receive the amount of such depreciation in other United States bonds at cash value, or in money, from the association receiving said bills, to be deposited with the Treasurer of the United States as long as such depreciation continues.

[And the Comptroller may permit the exchange of any of the bonds so deposited for other bonds of the United States, or the return of any of them upon the surrender and cancellation of a proportionate amount of the circulating notes; *provided*, the remaining bonds are sufficient for the requirements of this act, and the association has not failed to redeem its circulating notes.

Section 28 forbids any association to hold real estate, except such as may be necessary for its accommodation in its business, or may be mortgaged to it as security for debts previously contracted, or conveyed to it in satisfaction thereof, or may be purchased by it in order to secure debts due to it; or to hold possession under a mortgage, or to retain real estate purchased to secure debts, for more than five years.]

SEC. 29. *And be it further enacted,* That the total liabilities to any association, of any person, or of any company, corporation, or firm for money borrowed, including in the liabilities of a company or firm the liabilities of the several members thereof, shall at no time exceed one tenth part of the amount of the capital stock of such association actually paid in: *Provided,* that the discount of *bonâ fide* bills of exchange drawn against actually existing values, and the discount of commercial or business paper actually owned by the person or persons, corporation, or firm negotiating the same shall not be considered as money borrowed.

[Section 30 authorizes every association to charge upon loans or discounts made by it the rate of interest which the law of the State where it is established allows banks, organized under State laws, to charge; and, where no rate is fixed by the law of the State, to charge a rate not exceeding seven per cent. But the purchase or sale of a *bond fide* bill of exchange, payable at another place, at not more than the current rate of exchange in addition to the interest, shall not be considered as taking a greater rate of interest.]

SEC. 31. *And be it further enacted,* That every association in the cities hereinafter named shall, at all times, have on hand, in lawful money of the United States, an amount equal to at least twenty-five per centum of the aggregate amount of its notes in circulation and its deposits ; and every other association shall, at all times, have on hand, in lawful money of the United States, an amount equal to at least fifteen per centum of the aggregate amount of its notes in circulation, and of its deposits. And whenever the lawful money of any association in any of the cities hereinafter named shall be below the amount of twenty-five per centum of its circulation and deposits, and whenever the lawful money of any other association shall be below fifteen per centum of its circulation and deposits, such association shall not increase its liabilities by making any new loans or discounts otherwise than by discounting or purchasing bills of exchange payable at sight, nor make any dividend of its profits until the required proportion between the aggregate amount of its outstanding notes of circulation and deposits and its lawful money of the United States shall be restored : *Provided,* That three fifths of said fifteen per centum may consist of balances due to an association available for the redemption of its circulating notes from associations approved by the Comptroller of the Currency, organized under this act, in the cities of Saint Louis, Louisville, Chicago, Detroit, Milwaukie, New Orleans, Cincinnati, Cleveland, Pittsburg, Baltimore, Philadelphia, Boston, New York, Albany, Leavenworth, San Francisco, and Washington City : *Provided, also,* That clearing-house certificates, representing specie or lawful money specially deposited for the purpose of any clearing-house association, shall be deemed to be lawful money in the possession of any association belonging to such clearing-house holding and owning such certificate, and shall be considered to be a part of the lawful money which such association is required to have under the foregoing provisions of this section : *Provided,* That the cities of Charleston and Richmond

may be added to the list of cities in the national associations of which other associations may keep three fifths of their lawful money, whenever, in the opinion of the Comptroller of the Currency, the condition of the Southern States will warrant it. And it shall be competent for the Comptroller of the Currency to notify any association, whose lawful money reserve as aforesaid shall be below the amount to be kept on hand as aforesaid, to make good such reserve; and if such association shall fail for thirty days thereafter so to make good its reserve of lawful money of the United States, the Comptroller may, with the concurrence of the Secretary of the Treasury, appoint a receiver to wind up the business of such association, as provided in this act.

SEC. 32. *And be it further enacted,* That each association organized in any of the cities named in the foregoing section shall select, subject to the approval of the Comptroller of the Currency, an association in the city of New York, at which it will redeem its circulating notes at par. And each of such associations may keep one half of its lawful money reserve in cash deposits in the city of New York. And each association not organized within the cities named in the preceding section shall select, subject to the approval of the Comptroller of the Currency, an association in either of the cities named in the preceding section at which it will redeem its circulating notes at par, and the Comptroller shall give public notice of the names of the associations so selected at which redemptions are to be made by the respective associations, and of any change that may be made of the association at which the notes of any association are redeemed. If any association shall fail either to make the selection or to redeem its notes as aforesaid, the Comptroller of the Currency may, upon receiving satisfactory evidence thereof, appoint a receiver, in the manner provided for in this act, to wind up its affairs: *Provided,* That nothing in this section shall relieve any association from its liability to redeem its circulating notes at its own counter, at par, in lawful money, on demand: *And provided, further,* That every association formed or existing under the provisions of this act shall take and receive at par, for any debt or liability to said association, any and all notes or bills issued by any association existing under and by virtue of this act.

Sec. 33. *And be it further enacted*, That the directors of any association may, semi-annually, each year, declare a dividend of so much of the net profits of the association as they shall judge expedient; but each association shall, before the declaration of a dividend, carry one tenth part of its net profits of the preceding half year to its surplus fund until the same shall amount to twenty per centum of its capital stock.

[Section 34 provides for quarterly reports of the condition of every association, to be made by its officers to the Comptroller and published by him, and also for monthly reports to be made to him. This section was superseded by the Act of March 3, 1869, which directs that every association shall make at least five reports annually of its resources and liabilities on any past day specified by the Comptroller, and shall publish the same in a newspaper in the place where the association is established; and that every association shall also report to the Comptroller the amount of its net earnings and dividends, and make such further special reports as he may call for. 15 Statutes at Large, 326.]

Sec. 35. *And be it further enacted*, That no association shall make any loan or discount on the security of the shares of its own capital stock, nor be the purchaser or holder of any such shares, unless such security or purchase shall be necessary to prevent loss upon a debt previously contracted in good faith; and stock so purchased or acquired shall, within six months from the time of its purchase, be sold or disposed of at public or private sale, in default of which a receiver may be appointed to close up the business of the association, according to the provisions of this act.

Sec. 36. *And be it further enacted*, That no association shall at any time be indebted, or in any way liable, to an amount exceeding the amount of its capital stock at such time actually paid in and remaining undiminished by losses or otherwise, except on the following accounts, that is to say : —

First. On account of its notes of circulation.

Second. On account of moneys deposited with, or collected by, such association.

Third. On account of bills of exchange or drafts drawn

against money actually on deposit to the credit of such associa·
tion, or due thereto.

Fourth. On account of liabilities to its stockholders for dividends and reserved profits.

SEC. 37. *And be it further enacted,* That no association shall,
either directly or indirectly, pledge or hypothecate any of its
notes of circulation, for the purpose of procuring money to be
paid in on its capital stock, or to be used in its banking opera-
tions, or otherwise; nor shall any association use its circulating
notes, or any part thereof, in any manner or form, to create or
increase its capital stock.

[Section 38 forbids any association, while continuing its business, to
withdraw or permit to be withdrawn any of its capital, except as provided in section 13, or to make any dividend to an amount exceeding its
net profits then on hand, deducting therefrom its losses and bad debts;
and for this purpose all debts on which interest is past due and unpaid
for six months, unless they are well secured and in process of collection,
are to be held bad.

Section 39 forbids any association to pay out or put in circulation the
notes of any bank or association which are not at the time receivable at
par by the association paying them out; or to pay out or put in circulation the notes of any bank or association which is not redeeming its
notes in lawful money.]

SEC. 41. *And be it further enacted,* That the plates and special dies to be procured by the Comptroller of the Currency for
the printing of such circulating notes shall remain under his
control and direction, and the expenses necessarily incurred in
executing the provisions of this act respecting the procuring of
such notes, and all other expenses of the bureau, shall be paid
out of the proceeds of the taxes or duties now or hereafter to
be assessed on the circulation, and collected from associations
organized under this act.

[It is then provided that every association shall pay to the United
States a tax of one per cent. per annum on the average amount of its
notes in circulation, one half of one per cent. on the average amount of
its deposits, and one half of one per cent. on its capital stock beyond the
amount invested in United States bonds. But the shares of any association may be taxed as personal property by the State in which it is
located, and not elsewhere, at a rate not greater than is imposed upon
other moneyed capital in the hands of the citizens of the State, or upon

the shares of banks organized under the authority of the State; and the
real estate of associations shall be subject to State, county, and municipal taxes to the same extent as other real estate.

Section 42 provides for the closing of any association upon the vote
of shareholders owning two thirds of its capital, and for calling in its
notes. Under this section, as modified by the Act of July 14, 1870, any
association thus voting to close its affairs must within six months pay to
the Treasurer of the United States the amount of its outstanding notes
in lawful money; whereupon the bonds pledged as security for its circulation shall be returned to it, and its notes shall from that time be redeemed at the Treasury and destroyed, and the association discharged
from all liability therefor. 16 Statutes at Large, 274.

Section 44 provides that any bank established under the laws of any
State may by vote of the owners of two thirds of its capital stock be
reorganized as an association under this act, without change of stockholders or directors or in the amount of its shares, provided that its
capital shall not be less than is prescribed for associations under this
act.]

SEC. 45. *And be it further enacted*, That all associations
under this act, when designated for that purpose by the Secretary of the Treasury, shall be depositaries of public money, except receipts from customs, under such regulations as may be
prescribed by the Secretary; and they may also be employed as
financial agents of the government; and they shall perform all
such reasonable duties, as depositaries of public moneys and
financial agents of the government, as may be required of them.
And the Secretary of the Treasury shall require of the associations thus designated satisfactory security, by the deposit of
United States bonds and otherwise, for the safe-keeping and
prompt payment of the public money deposited with them, and
for the faithful performance of their duties as financial agents of
the government: *Provided*, that every association which shall
be selected and designated as receiver or depositary of the public money shall take and receive at par all of the national currency bills, by whatever association issued, which have been
paid in to the government for internal revenue, or for loans or
stocks.

[Section 46 *et seq.* provides that if any association shall fail to redeem
in lawful money any of its circulating notes, when payment thereof is
demanded at the proper place during the usual hours of business, the
holder of such notes may cause them to be protested and notify the

Comptroller of the failure. The Comptroller, if satisfied that the association has refused to pay its notes and is in default, shall declare the bonds pledged by the association to be forfeited to the United States and shall notify the holders of its notes to present them for payment at the Treasury. And for the notes thus paid at the Treasury, the Comptroller may either cancel an amount of the bonds equal at the market rate, not exceeding par, to the notes so paid, or may cause the necessary amount of the bonds to be sold by public auction in the city of New York, or may sell the necessary amount by private sale, provided that they shall not be sold by private sale for less than the market rate nor less than par. And if the proceeds of the bonds pledged by the association are insufficient to reimburse the amount expended in payment of its notes, the United States shall have a first and paramount lien for the deficiency upon all the assets of the association, to be made good in preference to all other claims.

Section 50 authorizes the Comptroller, when satisfied that any association has refused to pay its circulating notes and is in default, to appoint a receiver, who shall take charge of all the books and assets of the association and collect all debts and property belonging to it, and, if necessary, enforce the individual liability of the shareholders under section 12 of this act. And the Comptroller, after reimbursing to the United States, from the fund thus collected, any deficiency due from the association for the redemption of its notes, shall make a ratable payment of the debts of the association, and the remainder of the fund, if any, after payment of these debts, he shall pay over to the shareholders, in proportion to the stock held by each.]

SEC. 54. *And be it further enacted*, That the Comptroller of the Currency, with the approbation of the Secretary of the Treasury, as often as shall be deemed necessary or proper, shall appoint a suitable person or persons to make an examination of the affairs of every banking association, which person shall not be a director or other officer in any association whose affairs he shall be appointed to examine, and who shall have power to make a thorough examination into all the affairs of the association, and, in doing so, to examine any of the officers and agents thereof on oath; and shall make a full and detailed report of the condition of the association to the Comptroller.

[Succeeding sections provide penalties for embezzlement by the officers of any association, for the mutilation or disfigurement of notes with the intent to make them unfit for reissue, and for counterfeiting, passing counterfeit notes, or having in possession such notes or the engraved plates or paper for making such notes, with intent to use.

Section 61 requires the Comptroller to report annually to Congress the condition of every association as shown by its reports, with abstract statements of the total amount of liabilities, resources, and reserves, the amount of circulation redeemed and outstanding for associations which have closed their business during the year, and finally such changes in the laws relative to banking as may improve the system and increase its security.

Section 62 repeals the Act of February 25, 1863, but provides that the repeal shall not affect organizations or proceedings begun or had under said act, and that circulation issued by any association organized under it shall be deemed a part of the circulation authorized by the present act. And it is further provided that any association established or organizing under the former act may change its name, with the approval of the Comptroller.]

Sec. 63. *And be it further enacted,* That persons holding stock as executors, administrators, guardians, and trustees, shall not be personally subject to any liabilities as stockholders; but the estates and funds in their hands shall be liable in like manner and to the same extent as the testator, intestate, ward, or person interested in said trust-funds would be if they were respectively living and competent to act and hold the stock in their names.

Sec. 64. *And be it further enacted,* That Congress may at any time amend, alter, or repeal this act.

[By the Act of March 1, 1872, Leavenworth is struck out from the list of redemption cities in section 31 above. 17 Statutes at Large, 32.

The use of the word "national," as a part of the name of any bank not organized under the national currency act above, is forbidden by the Act of March 3, 1873. 17 Statutes at Large, 603.]

[Approved, June 3, 1864. 13 Statutes at Large, 99.]

Note. — The above act is in substance a revision of that of February 25, 1863, with only such changes as experience had shown to be necessary for the trial of the system. Some of the principal points of difference between the two acts are the following:—

The Act of 1863 made no provision for the redemption of the circulation by the banks of the principal cities, such as is contained in sections 31 and 32 of the Act of 1864; but simply required that every bank should redeem its circulation at its own counter, and that it should have for that and other purposes a reserve equal to twenty-five per cent. of its circulation and deposits, of which reserve three-fifths might be deposited with associations in nine principal cities named in the act.

The prohibition of the issue of circulating notes of a less denomina

tion than five dollars, contained in the Act of 1863, is removed by the Act of 1864.

The bonds deposited to secure the circulation under the Act of 1863, might be either coupon or registered, but by the Act of 1864 must be registered.

The Act of 1863 required a smaller minimum of capital for a new bank than the Act of 1864, required a smaller proportion to be paid in before beginning business, and allowed a longer time for the payment of the remainder.

The Act of 1864 makes more complete provision than that of 1863 for the conversion of State banks into national associations, permitting the retention of the former name of a bank after conversion, and in section 12 exempting the stockholders of such banks from personal liability under certain conditions, which were intended to meet the case of the Bank of Commerce in the city of New York. A section of the Act of 1863, authorizing any State bank holding United States bonds to the amount of one-half of its capital to issue circulating notes upon pledge and transfer of the bonds, is omitted in the Act of 1864.

The Act of 1863 failed to provide as to the taxation of shares by State authority.

The Act of 1863 required the apportionment of the total circulation among the States and Territories, one-half according to representative population and one-half having due regard to the existing banking capital and resources. This provision was omitted in the Act of 1864, but was revived in substance by the Act of March 3, 1865.

XVI ... June, 1864. — *An Act to prohibit certain Sales of Gold and Foreign Exchange.*

Be it enacted, . . . That it shall be unlawful to make any contract for the purchase or sale and delivery of any gold coin or bullion to be delivered on any day subsequent to the day of making such contract, or for the payment of any sum, either fixed or contingent, in default of the delivery of any gold coin or bullion, or to make such contract upon any other terms than the actual delivery of such gold coin or bullion, and the payment in full of the agreed price thereof, on the day on which such contract is made, in United States notes or national currency, and not otherwise; or to make any contract for the purchase or sale and delivery of any foreign exchange to be delivered at any time beyond ten days subsequent to the making of such contract; or for the payment of any sum, either fixed or contingent, in default of the delivery of any foreign exchange, or upon any other terms than the actual delivery of such foreign exchange within ten days from the making of such contract, and the immediate payment in full of the agreed price thereof on the day of de livery in United States notes or national currency; or to make any contract whatever for the sale and delivery of any gold coin or bullion of which the person making such contract shall not, at the time of making the same, be in actual possession. And it shall be unlawful to make any loan of money or currency not being in coin to be repaid in coin or bullion, or to make any loan of coin or bullion to be repaid in money or currency other than coin.

SEC. 2. *And be it further enacted,* That it shall be further unlawful for any banker, broker, or other person, to make any purchase or sale of any gold coin or bullion, or of any foreign exchange, or any contract for any such purchase or sale, at any other place than the ordinary place of business of either the seller or purchaser, owned or hired, and occupied by him individually, or by a partnership of which he is a member.

SEC. 3. *And be it further enacted,* That all contracts made in violation of this act shall be absolutely void.

SEC. 4. *And be it further enacted,* That any person who shall violate any provisions of this act shall be held guilty of a misdemeanor, and, on conviction thereof, be fined in any sum not less than one thousand dollars, nor more than ten thousand dollars, or be imprisoned for a period not less than three months, nor longer than one year, or both, at the discretion of the court, and shall likewise be subject to a penalty of one thousand dollars for each offence.

SEC. 5. *And be it further enacted,* That the penalties imposed by the fourth section of this act may be recovered in an action at law in any court of record of the United States, or any court of competent jurisdiction, which action may be brought in the name of the United States by any person who will sue for said penalty, one half for the use of the United States, and the other half for the use of the person bringing such action. And the recovery and satisfaction of a judgment in any such action shall be a bar to the imposition of any fine for the same offence in

any prosecution instituted subsequent to the recovery of such judgment, but shall not be a bar to the infliction of punishment by imprisonment, as provided by said fourth section.

Sec. 6. *And be it further enacted*, That all acts and parts of acts inconsistent with the provisions of this act are hereby repealed.

[Approved, June 17, 1864. 13 Statutes at Large, 132.]

Note. — The above act was repealed by the Act approved July 2, 1864. See 13 Statutes at Large, 844.

XVII.... June, 1864. — *An Act to provide Ways and Means for the Support of the Government, and for other Purposes.*

Be it enacted, ... That the Secretary of the Treasury be, and he is hereby, authorized to borrow, from time to time, on the credit of the United States, four hundred millions of dollars, and to issue therefor coupon or registered bonds of the United States, redeemable at the pleasure of the government, after any period not less than five, nor more than thirty, years, or, if deemed expedient, made payable at any period not more than forty years from date. And said bonds shall be of such denominations as the Secretary of the Treasury shall direct, not less than fifty dollars, and bear an annual interest not exceeding six per centum, payable semi-annually in coin. And the Secretary of the Treasury may dispose of such bonds, or any part thereof, and of any bonds commonly known as five-twenties remaining unsold, in the United States, or, if he shall find it expedient, in Europe, at any time, on such terms as he may deem most advisable, for lawful money of the United States, or, at his discretion, for treasury notes, certificates of indebtedness, or certificates of deposit issued under any act of Congress. And all bonds, treasury notes, and other obligations of the United States shall be exempt from taxation by or under State or municipal authority.

Sec. 2. *And be it further enacted*, That the Secretary of the Treasury may issue on the credit of the United States, and in lieu of an equal amount of bonds authorized by the preceding section, and as a part of said loan, not exceeding two hundred millions of dollars, in treasury notes of any denomination not less than ten dollars, payable at any time not exceeding three years from date, or, if thought more expedient, redeemable at any time after three years from date, and bearing interest not exceeding the rate of seven and three-tenths per centum, payable in lawful money at maturity, or, at the discretion of the Secretary, semi-annually. And the said treasury notes may be disposed of by the Secretary of the Treasury, on the best terms that can be obtained, for lawful money; and such of them as shall be made payable, principal and interest, at maturity, shall be a legal tender to the same extent as United States notes for their face value, excluding interest, and may be paid to any creditor of the United States at their face value, excluding interest, or to any creditor willing to receive them at par, including interest; and any treasury notes issued under the authority of this act may be made convertible, at the discretion of the Secretary of the Treasury, into any bonds issued under the authority of this act. And the Secretary of the Treasury may redeem, and cause to be cancelled and destroyed, any treasury notes or United States notes heretofore issued under authority of previous acts of Congress, and substitute, in lieu thereof, an equal amount of treasury notes such as are authorized by this act, or of other United States notes: *Provided*, That the total amount of bonds and treasury notes authorized by the first and second sections of this act shall not exceed four hundred millions of dollars, in addition to the amounts heretofore issued; nor shall the total amount of United States notes, issued or to be issued, ever exceed four hundred millions of dollars, and such additional sum, not exceeding fifty millions of dollars, as may be temporarily required for the redemption of temporary loan; nor shall any treasury note bearing interest, issued under this act, be a legal tender in payment or redemption of any notes issued by any bank, banking association, or banker, calculated or intended to circulate as money.

[Section 3 authorizes the Secretary of the Treasury to exchange bonds heretofore issued on which the interest is payable annually, for others bearing interest payable semi-annually. The treasury notes heretofore issued, bearing seven and three-tenths per cent. interest, may be exchanged for the six per cent. bonds heretofore authorized, at any time within three months after notice of redemption given by the Secretary, after which interest on such notes shall cease; and the interest on such notes after

maturity shall be paid in lawful money. So much of the Act of March 3, 1864, as limits the loan therein authorized to the current fiscal year, is repealed. The authority to issue bonds or notes, conferred by section 1 of the Act of March 3, 1863, is to cease on the passage of this act, except so far as it may affect seventy-five millions of bonds already advertised.]

SEC. 4. *And be it further enacted,* That the Secretary of the Treasury may authorize the receipt, as a temporary loan, of United States notes, or the notes of national banking associations, on deposit for not less than thirty days, in sums of not less than fifty dollars, by any of the Assistant Treasurers of the United States, or depositaries designated for that purpose, other than national banking associations, who shall issue certificates of deposit in such form as the Secretary of the Treasury shall prescribe, bearing interest not exceeding six per centum annually, and payable at any time after the term of deposit, and after ten days' subsequent notice, unless time and notice be waived by the Secretary of the Treasury; and the Secretary of the Treasury may increase the interest on deposits at less than six per centum to that rate, or, on ten days' notice to depositors, may diminish the rate of interest as the public interest may require; but the aggregate of such deposits shall not exceed one hundred and fifty millions of dollars; and the Secretary of the Treasury may issue, and shall hold in reserve for payment of such deposits, United States notes not exceeding fifty millions of dollars, including the amount already applied in such payment; and the United States notes, so held in reserve, shall be used only when needed, in his judgment, for the prompt payment of such deposits on demand, and shall be withdrawn and placed again in reserve as the amount of deposits shall again increase.

[Section 5 authorizes the Secretary of the Treasury to issue "notes of the fractions of a dollar as now used for currency," and to provide for their redemption when mutilated or defaced, and for their receipt in payment of debts to the United States, except for customs, in sums not over five dollars; and laws applicable to the fractional notes now authorized are made applicable to all fractional notes, postage currency, or postage stamps issued as currency, heretofore authorized; but the whole amount of all notes or stamps less than one dollar issued as currency shall not exceed fifty millions of dollars.]

[Approved, June 30, 1864. 13 Statutes at Large, 218.]

XVIII...January, 1865. — *An Act to amend an Act entitled "An Act to provide Ways and Means for the Support of the Government, and for other Purposes," approved June thirtieth, eighteen hundred and sixty-four.*

Be it enacted, ... That in lieu of any bonds authorized to be issued by the first section of the act entitled " An act to provide ways and means for the support of the government," approved June thirtieth, eighteen hundred and sixty-four, that may remain unsold at the date of this act, the Secretary of the Treasury may issue, under the authority of said act, treasury notes of the description and character authorized by the second section of said act: *Provided,* That the whole amount of bonds authorized as aforesaid, and treasury notes issued and to be issued in lieu thereof, shall not exceed the sum of four hundred millions of dollars; and such treasury notes may be disposed of for lawful money, or for any other treasury notes or certificates of indebtedness or certificates of deposit issued under any previous act of Congress; and such notes shall be exempt from taxation by or under State or municipal authority.

Sec. 2. *And be it further enacted,* That any bonds known as five-twenties, issued under the act of twenty-fifth February, eighteen hundred and sixty-two, remaining unsold to an amount not exceeding four millions of dollars, may be disposed of by the Secretary of the Treasury in the United States, or, if he shall find it expedient, in Europe, at any time, on such terms as he may deem most advisable: *Provided,* That this act shall not be so construed as to give any authority for the issue of any legal tender notes, in any form, beyond the balance unissued of the amount authorized by the second section of the act to which this is an amendment.

[Approved, January 28, 1865.　13 Statutes at Large, 425.]

XIX...March, 1865. — *An Act to provide Ways and Means for the Support of the Government.*

Be it enacted, ... That the Secretary of the Treasury be, and he is hereby, authorized to borrow, from time to time, on the credit of the United States, in addition to the amounts heretofore

authorized, any sums not exceeding in the aggregate six hundred
millions of dollars, and to issue therefor bonds or treasury notes
of the United States, in such form as he may prescribe; and so
much thereof as may be issued in bonds shall be of denominations not less than fifty dollars, and may be made payable at any
period not more than forty years from date of issue, or may be
made redeemable at the pleasure of the government, at or after
any period not less than five years nor more than forty years
from date, or may be made redeemable and payable as aforesaid,
as may be expressed upon their face; and so much thereof as may
be issued in treasury notes may be made convertible into any
bonds authorized by this act, and may be of such denominations
— not less than fifty dollars — and bear such dates, and be made
redeemable or payable at such periods as in the opinion of the
Secretary of the Treasury may be deemed expedient.   And the
interest on such bonds shall be payable semi-annually; and on
treasury notes authorized by this act the interest may be made
payable semi-annually, or annually, or at maturity thereof; and
the principal, or interest, or both, may be made payable in coin
or in other lawful money: *Provided*, That the rate of interest on
any such bonds or treasury notes, when payable in coin, shall not
exceed six per centum per annum; and when not payable in coin
shall not exceed seven and three-tenths per centum per annum;
and the rate and character of interest shall be expressed on all
such bonds or treasury notes: *And provided, further*, That the
act entitled "An act to provide ways and means for the support
of the government, and for other purposes," approved June thirtieth, eighteen hundred and sixty-four, shall be so construed as to
authorize the issue of bonds of any description authorized by this
act.   And any treasury notes or other obligations bearing interest, issued under any act of Congress, may, at the discretion of
the Secretary of the Treasury, and with the consent of the
holder, be converted into any description of bonds authorized by
this act; and no bonds so authorized shall be considered a part
of the amount of six hundred millions hereinbefore authorized.

[Section 2 authorizes the Secretary of the Treasury to dispose of any
of the obligations issued under this act, where and under such condition,
and at such rates as he thinks best, for coin or other lawful money,

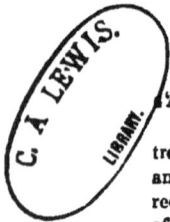

treasury notes, or certificates of indebtedness or of deposit, and the like; and to issue bonds or treasury notes authorized by this act in payment of requisitions for materials or supplies, on receiving notice that the owner of the claim for which any requisition is made desires to subscribe for a portion of the loan; "and all bonds or other obligations issued under this act shall be exempt from taxation by or under state or municipal authority."

Section 8 contains a proviso, " That nothing herein contained shall be construed as authorizing the issue of legal-tender notes in any form."]

[Approved, March 3, 1865.   13 Statutes at Large, 468.]

XX.... March, 1865. — *An Act to amend an Act entitled " An Act to provide Internal Revenue to support the Government, to pay Interest on the Public Debt, and for other Purposes," approved June thirtieth, eighteen hundred and sixty-four.*

SEC. 6. *And be it further enacted,* That every national banking association, State bank, or State banking association, shall pay a tax of ten per centum on the amount of notes of any State bank or State banking association, paid out by them after the first day of July, eighteen hundred and sixty-six.

[Section 9 of the act to reduce internal taxation, approved July 13, 1866, includes the notes "of any person" among those to be taxed as above.   13 Statutes at Large, 146.

Section 2 of "An act to exempt wrapping paper, made from wood or cornstalks, from internal tax, and for other purposes," approved, March 26, 1867, includes also the notes of any town, city, or municipal corporation among those to be taxed as above.   15 Statutes at Large, 6.]

SEC. 7. *And be it further enacted,* That any existing bank organized under the laws of any State, having a paid-up capital of not less than seventy-five thousand dollars, which shall apply before the first day of July next for authority to become a national bank under the act entitled " An act to provide a national currency secured by a pledge of United States bonds, and to provide for the circulation and redemption thereof," approved June third, eighteen hundred and sixty-four, and shall comply with all the requirements of said act, shall, if such bank be found by the Comptroller of the Currency to be in good standing and credit, receive such authority in preference to new associations applying for the same. . . .

[Approved, March 3, 1865.   13 Statutes at Large, 469.]

XXI. ... March, 1865. — *An Act to amend an Act entitled " An Act to provide a National Currency, secured by a Pledge of United States Bonds, and to provide for the Circulation and Redemption thereof."*

Be it enacted, . . . That section twenty-one of said act be so amended that said section shall read as follows :

[In lieu of the concluding sentence of said section "and at no time shall the total amount of such notes . . . exceed the amount . . . of its capital stock" the following is substituted :]

. . . and the amount of said circulating notes to be furnished to each association shall be in proportion to its paid-up capital as follows, and no more : To each association whose capital shall not exceed five hundred thousand dollars, ninety per centum of such capital ; to each association whose capital exceeds five hundred thousand dollars, but does not exceed one million dollars, eighty per centum of such capital ; to each association whose capital exceeds one million dollars, but does not exceed three millions of dollars, seventy-five per centum of such capital ; to each association whose capital exceeds three millions of dollars, sixty per centum of such capital. And that one hundred and fifty millions of dollars of the entire amount of circulating notes authorized to be issued shall be apportioned to associations in the States, in the District of Columbia, and in the Territories, according to representative population, and the remainder shall be apportioned by the Secretary of the Treasury among associations formed in the several States, in the District of Columbia, and in the Territories, having due regard to the existing banking capital, resources, and business of such States, District, and Territories.

[Approved, March 3, 1865. 13 Statutes at Large, 498.]

XXII. ... April, 1866. — *An Act to amend an Act entitled " An Act to provide Ways and Means to support the Government," approved March third, eighteen hundred and sixty-five.*

Be it enacted, . . . That the act entitled " An act to provide ways and means to support the Government," approved March third, eighteen hundred and sixty-five, shall be extended and construed to authorize the Secretary of the Treasury, at his discretion, to receive any treasury notes or other obligations issued under any act of Congress, whether bearing interest or not, in exchange for any description of bonds authorized by the act to which this is an amendment; and also to dispose of any description of bonds authorized by said act, either in the United States or elsewhere, to such an amount, in such manner, and at such rates as he may think advisable, for lawful money of the United States, or for any treasury notes, certificates of indebtedness, or certificates of deposit, or other representatives of value, which have been or which may be issued under any act of Congress, the proceeds thereof to be used only for retiring treasury notes or other obligations issued under any act of Congress; but nothing herein contained shall be construed to authorize any increase of the public debt: *Provided,* That of United States notes not more than ten millions of dollars may be retired and cancelled within six months from the passage of this act, and thereafter not more than four millions of dollars in any one month: *And provided further,* That the act to which this is an amendment shall continue in full force in all its provisions, except as modified by this act.

[Approved, April 12, 1866. 14 Statutes at Large, 81.]

Note. — The following resolution was adopted by the House of Representatives, December 18, 1865: —

"*Resolved,* That this House cordially concurs in the views of the Secretary of the Treasury in relation to the necessity of a contraction of the currency with a view to as early a resumption of specie payments as the business interests of the country will permit; and we hereby pledge coöperative action to this end as speedily as possible."

[Congressional Globe, December, 1865, p. 75.]

XXIII ... March, 1867. — *An Act to provide Ways and Means for the Payment of Compound Interest Notes.*

[This act directs the Secretary of the Treasury, for the purpose of redeeming any outstanding compound interest notes, to issue temporary loan certificates as prescribed by section 4 of the act of February 25, 1862, bearing interest not exceeding three per cent. per annum, and principal and interest payable in lawful money on demand; the amount of certificates at any time outstanding not to exceed fifty millions of dollars.

And said certificates may be held by any national bank as part of the reserve required by sections 31 and 32 of the National Currency Act of June 3, 1864; but not less than two-fifths of the entire reserve of such bank shall consist of lawful money.]

[Approved, March 2, 1867.   14 Statutes at Large, 558.]

XXIV.... February, 1868. — *An Act to suspend further Reduction of the Currency.*

Be it enacted, . . . That from and after the passage of this act, the authority of the Secretary of the Treasury to make any reduction of the currency, by retiring or cancelling United States notes, shall be, and is hereby, suspended; but nothing herein contained shall prevent the cancellation and destruction of mutilated United States notes, and the replacing of the same with notes of the same character and amount.

NOTE. — The above act having been presented to the President of the United States for his approval, and not having been returned by him to the House of Congress in which it originated within the time prescribed by the Constitution, became a law without his approval, February 4, 1868.

[15 Statutes at Large, 34.]

XXV.... July, 1868. — *An Act to provide for a further Issue of temporary Loan Certificates, for the Purpose of redeeming and retiring the Remainder of the outstanding Compound Interest Notes.*

[For the sole purpose of redeeming the remainder of the compound interest notes, this act adds twenty-five millions of dollars to the amount of three per cent. temporary loan certificates authorized by the act of March 2, 1867.]

[Approved, July 25, 1868.   15 Statutes at Large, 183.]

XXVI... February, 1869. — *An Act to prevent loaning Money upon United States Notes.*

Be it enacted, . . . That no national banking association shall hereafter offer or receive United States notes or national bank notes as security or as collateral security for any loan of money, or for a consideration shall agree to withhold the same from use, or shall offer or receive the custody or promise of custody of such notes as security, or as collateral security, or consideration for any loan of money. . . .

[Approved, February 19, 1869. 15 Statutes at Large, 270.]

XXVII. . . . March, 1869. — *An Act to strengthen the Public Credit.*

Be it enacted, . . . That in order to remove any doubt as to the purpose of the government to discharge all just obligations to the public creditors, and to settle conflicting questions and interpretations of the laws by virtue of which such obligations have been contracted, it is hereby provided and declared that the faith of the United States is solemnly pledged to the payment in coin or its equivalent of all the obligations of the United States not bearing interest, known as United States notes, and of all the interest-bearing obligations of the United States, except in cases where the law authorizing the issue of any such obligation has expressly provided that the same may be paid in lawful money or other currency than gold or silver. But none of said interest-bearing obligations not already due shall be redeemed or paid before maturity unless at such time United States notes shall be convertible into coin at the option of the holder, or unless at such time bonds of the United States bearing a lower rate of interest than the bonds to be redeemed can be sold at par in coin. And the United States also solemnly pledges its faith to make provision at the earliest practicable period for the redemption of the United States notes in coin.

[Approved, March 18, 1869. 16 Statutes at Large, 1.]

XXVIII. . . . July, 1870. — *An Act to provide for the Redemption of the three per cent. temporary Loan Certificates, and for an Increase of National Bank Notes.*

Be it enacted, . . . That fifty-four millions of dollars in notes for circulation may be issued to national banking associations, in addition to the three hundred millions of dollars authorized by the twenty-second section of the "Act to provide a national currency, secured by a pledge of United States bonds, and to provide for the circulation and redemption thereof," approved

June three, eighteen hundred and sixty-four; and the amount
of notes so provided shall be furnished to banking associations
organized or to be organized in those States and Territories
having less than their proportion under the apportionment contemplated by the provisions of the "Act to amend an act to
provide a national currency, secured by a pledge of United
States bonds, and to provide for the circulation and redemption
thereof," approved March three, eighteen hundred and sixty-
five, and the bonds deposited with the Treasurer of the United
States, to secure the additional circulating notes herein authorized, shall be of any description of bonds of the United States
bearing interest in coin, but a new apportionment of the increased circulation herein provided for shall be made as soon as
practicable, based upon the census of eighteen hundred and seventy: *Provided,* That if applications for the circulation herein
authorized shall not be made within one year after the passage
of this act by banking associations organized or to be organized
in States having less than their proportion, it shall be lawful for
the Comptroller of the Currency to issue such circulation to
banking associations applying for the same in other States or
Territories having less than their proportion, giving the preference to such as have the greatest deficiency: *And providea
further,* That no banking association hereafter organized shall
have a circulation in excess of five hundred thousand dollars.

[Section 2 provides that at the end of every month the Secretary of
the Treasury shall call in and redeem an amount of the three per cent.
temporary loan certificates issued under the Acts of March 2, 1867, and
July 25, 1868, not less than the amount of circulating notes issued to national banking associations under the preceding section during the previous month.]

Sec. 3. *And be it further enacted,* That upon the deposit of
any United States bonds, bearing interest payable in gold, with
the Treasurer of the United States, in the manner prescribed in
the nineteenth and twentieth sections of the national currency
act, it shall be lawful for the Comptroller of the Currency to
issue to the association making the same, circulating notes of
different denominations, not less than five dollars, not exceeding
in amount eighty per centum of the par value of the bonds de-

posited, which notes shall bear upon their face the promise of
the association to which they are issued to pay them, upon presentation at the office of the association, in gold coin of the
United States, and shall be redeemable upon such presentation
in such coin : *Provided*, That no banking association organized
under this section shall have a circulation in excess of one million of dollars.

SEC. 4. *And be it further enacted*, That every national banking association formed under the provisions of the preceding
section of this act shall at all times keep on hand not less than
twenty-five per centum of its outstanding circulation in gold or
silver coin of the United States, and shall receive at par in the
payment of debts the gold notes of every other such banking
association which at the time of such payments shall be redeeming its circulating notes in gold coin of the United States.

SEC. 5. *And be it further enacted*, That every association organized for the purpose of issuing gold notes as provided in this
act shall be subject to all the requirements and provisions of the
national currency act, except the first clause of section twenty-
two, which limits the circulation of national banking associations
to three hundred millions of dollars; the first clause of section
thirty-two, which, taken in connection with the preceding section,
would require national banking associations organized in the
city of San Francisco to redeem their circulating notes at par
in the city of New York; and the last clause of section thirty-
two, which requires every national banking association to receive in payment of debts the notes of every other national
banking association at par: *Provided*, That in applying the provisions and requirements of said act to the banking associations
herein provided for, the terms "lawful money," and "lawful
money of the United States," shall be held and construed to
mean gold or silver coin of the United States.

SEC. 6. *And be it further. enacted*, That to secure a more
equitable distribution of the national banking currency there
may be issued circulating notes to banking associations organized
in States and Territories having less than their proportion as
herein set forth. And the amounts of circulation in this section
authorized shall, under the direction of the Secretary of the

Treasury, as it may be required for this purpose, be withdrawn, as herein provided, from banking associations organized in States having a circulation exceeding that provided for by the act entitled " An act to amend an act entitled ' An act to provide for a national banking currency, secured by pledge of United States bonds, and to provide for the circulation and redemption thereof,' " approved March three, eighteen hundred and sixty-five, but the amount so withdrawn shall not exceed twenty-five million dollars.

[It is then provided that the redistribution shall be made, when required, by withdrawing from banks having a circulation exceeding one million dollars such excess, in States having more than their proportion; and then from banks having a circulation exceeding three hundred thousand dollars their excess over that amount, beginning with States having the largest proportion in excess, and proceeding, if necessary, to those having a smaller proportion. Upon the failure of any association to retire the amount of its circulation required as above, the Comptroller of the Currency is authorized to sell the necessary amount of its bonds and to redeem its notes to the amount required. But no circulation is to be withdrawn under this section until the fifty-four millions granted in section 1 shall have been taken up.

Section 7 provides that after six months from the passage of this act any association may be removed from any State having more than its proportion of circulation to any State having less than its proportion; but the amount of the issue of said association shall not be deducted from the new issue herein provided for.]

[Approved, July 12, 1870. 16 Statutes at Large, 251.].

XXIX.... July, 1870. — *An Act to authorize the Refunding of the National Debt.*

Be it enacted, . . . That the Secretary of the Treasury is hereby authorized to issue, in a sum or sums not exceeding in the aggregate two hundred million dollars, coupon or registered bonds of the United States, in such form as he may prescribe, and of denominations of fifty dollars, or some multiple of that sum, redeemable in coin of the present standard value, at the pleasure of the United States, after ten years from the date of their issue, and bearing interest, payable semi-annually in such coin, at the rate of five per cent. per annum; also a sum or sums not exceeding in the aggregate three hundred million dollars of

4

like bonds, the same in all respects, but payable at the pleasure
of the United States, after fifteen years from the date of their
issue, and bearing interest at the rate of four and a half per
cent. per annum; also a sum or sums not exceeding in the
aggregate one thousand million dollars of like bonds, the same
in all respects, but payable at the pleasure of the United States,
after thirty years from the date of their issue, and bearing interest at the rate of four per cent. per annum; all of which said
several classes of bonds and the interest thereon shall be exempt from the payment of all taxes or duties of the United
States, as well as from taxation in any form by or under
State, municipal, or local authority; and the said bonds shall
have set forth and expressed upon their face the above-specified
conditions, and shall, with their coupons, be made payable at the
Treasury of the United States. But nothing in this act, or in
any other law now in force, shall be construed to authorize any
increase whatever of the bonded debt of the United States.

[By the amendatory Act of January 20, 1871, the amount of bonds
to be issued bearing interest at five per cent. is increased to five hundred
millions of dollars, but without any increase of the total amount of bonds
provided for above; and the Secretary of the Treasury is authorized to
make the interest of any of the bonds so provided for payable quarter-
yearly. 16 Statutes at Large, 399.]

SEC. 2. *And be it further enacted,* That the Secretary of the
Treasury is hereby authorized to sell and dispose of any of the
bonds issued under this act, at not less than their par value for
coin, and to apply the proceeds thereof to the redemption of any
of the bonds of the United States outstanding, and known as five-
twenty bonds, at their par value, or he may exchange the same
for such five-twenty bonds, par for par; but the bonds hereby
authorized shall be used for no other purpose whatsoever. And
a sum not exceeding one-half of one per cent. of the bonds
herein authorized is hereby appropriated to pay the expense of
preparing, issuing, advertising, and disposing of the same.

[Section 4 authorizes the Secretary of the Treasury, with any coin
that is lawfully applicable, to pay at par and cancel any of the five-
twenty bonds that may become redeemable by the terms of their issue;
the particular bonds so to be paid to be called for by public notice speci-

fying their class, date and number, and interest on them to cease in three months after the date of such notice.]

SEC. 5. *And be it further enacted,* That the Secretary of the Treasury is hereby authorized, at any time within two years from the passage of this act, to receive gold coin of the United States on deposit for not less than thirty days, in sums of not less than one hundred dollars, with the Treasurer, or any Assistant Treasurer of the United States authorized by the Secretary of the Treasury to receive the same, who shall issue therefor certificates of deposit, made in such form as the Secretary of the Treasury shall prescribe, and said certificates of deposit shall bear interest at a rate not exceeding two and a half per cent. per annum; and any amount of gold coin so deposited may be withdrawn from deposit at any time after thirty days from the date of deposit, and after ten days' notice and on the return of said certificates: *Provided,* That the interest on all such deposits shall cease and determine at the pleasure of the Secretary of the Treasury. And not less than twenty-five per cent. of the coin deposited for or represented by said certificates of deposits shall be retained in the treasury for the payment of said certificates; and the excess beyond twenty-five per cent. may be applied at the discretion of the Secretary of the Treasury to the payment or redemption of such outstanding bonds of the United States heretofore issued and known as the five-twenty bonds, as he may designate under the provisions of the fourth section of this act; and any certificates of deposit issued as aforesaid, may be received at par with the interest accrued thereon in payment for any bonds authorized to be issued by this act.

SEC. 6. *And be it further enacted,* That the United States bonds purchased and now held in the treasury in accordance with the provisions relating to a sinking fund, of section five of the act entitled "An act to authorize the issue of United States notes, and for the redemption or funding thereof, and for funding the floating debt of the United States," approved February twenty-fifth, eighteen hundred and sixty-two, and all other United States bonds which have been purchased by the Secretary of the Treasury with surplus funds in the treasury, and now held in the Treasury of the United States, shall be cancelled

and destroyed, a detailed record of such bonds so cancelled and
destroyed to be first made in the books of the Treasury Department. Any bonds hereafter applied to said sinking fund, and
all other United States bonds redeemed or paid hereafter by the
United States, shall also in like manner be recorded, cancelled
and destroyed, and the amount of the bonds of each class that
have been cancelled and destroyed shall be deducted respectively
from the amount of each class of the outstanding debt of the
United States. In addition to other amounts that may be applied
to the redemption or payment of the public debt, an amount equal
to the interest on all bonds belonging to the aforesaid sinking
fund shall be applied, as the Secretary of the Treasury shall from
time to time direct, to the payment of the public debt as provided for in section five of the act aforesaid. And the amount
so to be applied is hereby appropriated annually for that purpose, out of the receipts for duties on imported goods.

[Approved, July 14, 1870. 16 Statutes at Large, 272]

XXX ...June, 1872. — *An Act for the better Security of Bank
Reserves, and to facilitate Bank Clearing-house Exchanges.*

Be it enacted, . . . That the Secretary of the Treasury is
hereby authorized to receive United States notes on deposit,
without interest, from national banking associations, in sums not
less than ten thousand dollars, and to issue certificates therefor
in such form as the secretary may prescribe, in denominations
of not less than five thousand dollars; which certificate shall be
payable on demand in United States notes, at the place where
the deposits were made.

SEC. 2. That the United States notes so deposited in the
Treasury of the United States shall not be counted as part of
the legal reserve; but the certificates issued therefor may be
held and counted by national banks as part of their legal reserve, and may be accepted in the settlement of clearing-house
balances at the places where the deposits therefor were made.

SEC. 3. That nothing contained in this act shall be construed
to authorize any expansion or contraction of the currency; and
the United States notes for which such certificates are issued, or
other United States notes of like amount, shall be held as spe-

cial deposits in the treasury, and used only for the redemption of such certificates.

[Approved, June 8, 1872.   17 Statutes at Large, 336.]

XXXI ... June, 1874. — *An Act fixing the Amount of United States Notes, providing for a Redistribution of the National Bank Currency, and for other Purposes.*

Be it enacted, . . . That the act entitled " An act to provide a national currency secured by a pledge of United States bonds, and to provide for the circulation and redemption thereof," approved June third, eighteen hundred and sixty-four, shall be hereafter known as " the national bank act."

SEC. 2. That section thirty-one of the " national bank act " be so amended that the several associations therein provided for shall not hereafter be required to keep on hand any amount of money whatever, by reason of the amount of their respective circulations; but the moneys required by said section to be kept at all times on hand shall be determined by the amount of deposits in all respects, as provided for in the said section.

SEC. 3. That every association organized, or to be organized, under the provisions of the said act, and of the several acts amendatory thereof, shall at all times keep and have on deposit in the Treasury of the United States, in lawful money of the United States, a sum equal to five per centum of its circulation, to be held and used for the redemption of such circulation; which sum shall be counted as a part of its lawful reserve, as provided in section two of this act; and when the circulating notes of any such associations, assorted or unassorted, shall be presented for redemption, in sums of one thousand dollars, or any multiple thereof, to the Treasurer of the United States, the same shall be redeemed in United States notes. All notes so redeemed shall be charged by the Treasurer of the United States to the respective associations issuing the same, and he shall notify them severally, on the first day of each month, or oftener, at his discretion, of the amount of such redemptions; and whenever such redemptions for any association shall amount to the sum of five hundred dollars, such association so notified shall forthwith deposit with the Treasurer of the United States a sum in United States notes equal to the amount of its circulating notes so redeemed. And all notes of national banks worn, defaced, mutilated, or otherwise unfit for circulation shall, when received by any Assistant Treasurer or at any designated depository of the United States, be forwarded to the Treasurer of the United States for redemption as provided herein. And when such redemptions have been so reimbursed, the circulating notes so redeemed shall be forwarded to the respective associations by which they were issued; but if any of such notes are worn, mutilated, defaced, or rendered otherwise unfit for use, they shall be forwarded to the Comptroller of the Currency and destroyed and replaced as now provided by law : *Provided,* That each of said associations shall reimburse to the treasury the charges for transportation, and the costs for assorting such notes ; and the associations hereafter organized shall also severally reimburse to the treasury the cost of engraving such plates as shall be ordered by each association respectively; and the amount assessed upon each association shall be in proportion to the circulation redeemed, and be charged to the fund on deposit with the Treasurer: *And provided further,* That so much of section thirty-two of said national bank act requiring or permitting the redemption of its circulating notes elsewhere than at its own counter, except as provided for in this section, is hereby repealed.

SEC. 4. That any association organized under this act, or any of the acts of which this is an amendment, desiring to withdraw its circulating notes, in whole or in part, may, upon the deposit of lawful money with the Treasurer of the United States in sums of not less than nine thousand dollars, take up the bonds which said association has on deposit with the Treasurer for the security of such circulating notes; which bonds shall be assigned to the bank in the manner specified in the nineteenth section of the national bank act; and the outstanding notes of said association, to an amount equal to the legal tender notes deposited, shall be redeemed at the Treasury of the United States, and destroyed as now provided by law : *Provided,* That the amount of the bonds on deposit for circulation shall not be reduced below fifty thousand dollars.

SEC. 5. That the Comptroller of the Currency shall, under such rules and regulations as the Secretary of the Treasury may prescribe, cause the charter numbers of the association to be printed upon all national bank notes which may be hereafter issued by him.

SEC. 6. That the amount of United States notes outstanding and to be used as a part of the circulating medium, shall not exceed the sum of three hundred and eighty-two million dollars, which said sum shall appear in each monthly statement of the public debt, and no part thereof shall be held or used as a reserve.

SEC. 7. That so much of the act entitled "An act to provide for the redemption of the three per centum temporary loan certificates, and for an increase of national bank notes," as provides that no circulation shall be withdrawn under the provisions of section six of said act, until after the fifty-four millions granted in section one of said act shall have been taken up, is hereby repealed; and it shall be the duty of the Comptroller of the Currency, under the direction of the Secretary of the Treasury, to proceed forthwith, and he is hereby authorized and required, from time to time, as applications shall be duly made therefor, and until the full amount of fifty-five million dollars shall be withdrawn, to make requisitions upon each of the national banks described in said section, and in the manner therein provided, organized in States having an excess of circulation, to withdraw and return so much of their circulation as by said act may be apportioned to be withdrawn from them, or, in lieu thereof, to deposit in the Treasury of the United States lawful money sufficient to redeem such circulation, and upon the return of the circulation required, or the deposit of lawful money, as herein provided, a proportionate amount of the bonds held to secure the circulation of such association as shall make such return or deposit shall be surrendered to it.

SEC. 8. That upon the failure of the national banks upon which requisition for circulation shall be made, or of any of them, to return the amount required, or to deposit in the Treasury lawful money to redeem the circulation required, within thirty days, the Comptroller of the Currency shall at once sell as pro-

vided in section forty-nine of the national currency act, approved
June third, eighteen hundred and sixty-four, bonds held to secure
the redemption of the circulation of the association or associations which shall so fail, to an amount sufficient to redeem the
circulation required of such association or associations, and with
the proceeds, which shall be deposited in the Treasury of the
United States, so much of the circulation of such association or
associations shall be redeemed as will equal the amount required
and not returned, and if there be any excess of proceeds over
the amount required for such redemption, it shall be returned to
the association or associations whose bonds shall have been sold.
And it shall be the duty of the Treasurer, Assistant Treasurers,
designated depositaries, and national bank depositaries of the
United States, who shall be kept informed by the Comptroller
of the Currency of such associations as shall fail to return circulation as required, to assort and return to the Treasury for redemption the notes of such associations as shall come into their hands
until the amount required shall be redeemed, and in like manner
to assort and return to the Treasury, for redemption, the notes
of such national banks as have failed, or gone into voluntary
liquidation for the purpose of winding up their affairs, and of
such as shall hereafter so fail or go into liquidation.

SEC. 9. That from and after the passage of this act it shall
be lawful for the Comptroller of the Currency, and he is hereby
required, to issue circulating notes, without delay, as applications
therefor are made, not to exceed the sum of fifty-five million
dollars, to associations organized, or to be organized, in those
States and Territories having less than their proportion of circulation, under an apportionment made on the basis of population
and of wealth, as shown by the returns of the census of eighteen
hundred and seventy ; and every association hereafter organized
shall be subject to, and be governed by the rules, restrictions,
and limitations, and possess the rights, privileges, and franchises,
now or hereafter to be prescribed by law as to national banking
associations, with the same power to amend, alter, and repeal
provided by " the national bank act:" *Provided,* That the whole
amount of circulation withdrawn and redeemed from banks trans-
acting business shall not exceed fifty-five million dollars, and

Resumption Act of January '75 providing for Specie

that such circulation shall be withdrawn and redeemed as it shall
be necessary to supply the circulation previously issued to the
banks in those States having less than their apportionment : *And
provided further*, That not more than thirty million dollars shall
be withdrawn and redeemed as herein contemplated during the
fiscal year ending June thirtieth, eighteen hundred and seventy-
five.

[Approved, June 20, 1874. 18 Statutes at Large, 123.]

XXXII.... January, 1875. — *An Act to provide for the Resumption of Specie Payments.*

Be it enacted, . . . That the Secretary of the Treasury is
hereby authorized and required, as rapidly as practicable, to
cause to be coined at the mints of the United States, silver coins
of the denominations of ten, twenty-five, and fifty cents, of
standard value, and to issue them in redemption of an equal
number and amount of fractional currency of similar denominations, or, at his discretion, he may issue such silver coins through
the mints, the subtreasuries, public depositaries, and post-offices
of the United States ; and, upon such issue, he is hereby authorized and required to redeem an equal amount of such fractional
currency, until the whole amount of such fractional currency
outstanding shall be redeemed.

[An act approved April 17, 1876, makes further provision for the
issue of silver coin in redemption of fractional currency, and also provides that the fractional currency so redeemed shall be held to be a part
of the sinking-fund, and that interest shall be computed thereon, as in
the case of bonds belonging to the sinking-fund. See 19 Statutes at
Large, 33.]

SEC. 2. That so much of section three thousand five hundred and twenty-four of the Revised Statutes of the United
States as provides for a charge of one-fifth of one per centum
for converting standard gold bullion into coin is hereby repealed,
and hereafter no charge shall be made for that service.

SEC. 3. That section five thousand one hundred and seventy-
seven of the Revised Statutes of the United States, limiting the
aggregate amount of circulating notes of national banking associations, be, and is hereby, repealed; and each existing banking
association may increase its circulating notes in accordance with

existing law without respect to said aggregate limit; and new banking associations may be organized in accordance with existing law without respect to said aggregate limit; and the provisions of law for the withdrawal and redistribution of national bank currency among the several States and Territories are hereby repealed. And whenever, and so often, as circulating notes shall be issued to any such banking association, so increasing its capital or circulating notes, or so newly organized as aforesaid, it shall be the duty of the Secretary of the Treasury to redeem the legal tender United States notes in excess only of three hundred millions of dollars, to the amount of eighty per centum of the sum of national bank notes so issued to any such banking association as aforesaid, and to continue such redemption as such circulating notes are issued until there shall be outstanding the sum of three hundred million dollars of such legal tender United States notes, and no more. And on and after the first day of January, anno Domini eighteen hundred and seventy-nine, the Secretary of the Treasury shall redeem, in coin, the United States legal tender notes then outstanding on their presentation for redemption, at the office of the Assistant Treasurer of the United States in the city of New York, in sums of not less than fifty dollars. And to enable the Secretary of the Treasury to prepare and provide for the redemption in this act authorized or required, he is authorized to use any surplus revenues, from time to time, in the Treasury not otherwise appropriated, and to issue, sell, and dispose of, at not less than par, in coin, either of the descriptions of bonds of the United States described in the Act of Congress approved July fourteenth, eighteen hundred and seventy, entitled, "An Act to authorize the refunding of the national debt," with like qualities, privileges, and exemptions, to the extent necessary to carry this act into full effect, and to use the proceeds thereof for the purposes aforesaid. And all provisions of law inconsistent with the provisions of this act are hereby repealed.

[The limit of circulation fixed by section 5177 of the Revised Statutes is that prescribed on page 46 by section 1 of the Act of July 12, 1870.]

[Approved, January 14, 1875. 18 Statutes at Large, 296.]

XXXIII....January, 1875. — *An Act to remove the Limitation restricting the Circulation of Banking Associations issuing Notes payable in Gold.*

Be it enacted, . . . That so much of section five thousand one hundred and eighty-five of the Revised Statutes of the United States as limits the circulation of banking associations, organized for the purpose of issuing notes payable in gold, severally to one million dollars, be, and the same is hereby, repealed; and each of such existing banking associations may increase its circulating notes, and new banking associations may be organized, in accordance with existing law, without respect to such limitation.

[Approved, January 19, 1875.   18 Statutes at Large, 302.]

[The limit of circulation fixed by section 5185 of the Revised Statutes is that prescribed on page 48, by section 3 of the Act of July 12, 1870.]

XXXIV....March, 1875. — *An Act making Appropriations for sundry Civil Expenses of the Government for the fiscal year ending June thirtieth, eighteen hundred and seventy-six, and for other purposes.*

SEC. 11. That the Secretary of the Treasury is hereby authorized, at such times as may be necessary, for the purpose of obtaining bonds for the sinking-fund, in compliance with sections three thousand six hundred and ninety-four to three thousand six hundred and ninety-seven, inclusive, of the Revised Statutes of the United States, to give public notice that he will redeem, in coin, at par, any bonds of the United States, bearing interest at the rate of six per centum, of the kind known as five-twenties; and in three months after the date of such public notice, the interest on the bonds so selected and called for payment shall cease.

[Approved, March 3, 1875.   18 Statutes at Large, 401.]

[The provisions of sections 3694-97 of the Revised Statutes are the same as those of section 5 of the Act of February 25, 1862, on page 12, and section 6 of the Act of July 14, 1870, on page 51.]

XXXV. . . . May, 1878. — *An Act to forbid the further retirement of United States legal-tender notes.*

Be it enacted, . . . That from and after the passage of this act it shall not be lawful for the Secretary of the Treasury or other officer under him to cancel or retire any more of the United States legal-tender notes.   And when any of said notes may be redeemed or be received into the Treasury under any law from any source whatever and shall belong to the United States, they shall not be retired cancelled or destroyed but they shall be reissued and paid out again and kept in circulation : *Provided,* That nothing herein shall prohibit the cancellation and destruction of mutilated notes and the issue of other notes of like denomination in their stead, as now provided by law.

All acts and parts of acts in conflict herewith are hereby repealed.

[Approved, May 31, 1878.   20 Statutes at Large, 87.]

XXXVI. . . . January, 1879. — *An Act to facilitate the refunding the national debt.*

Be it enacted, . . . That the Secretary of the Treasury is hereby authorized in the process of refunding the national debt under existing laws to exchange directly at par the bonds of the United States bearing interest at four per centum per annum authorized by law for the bonds of the United States commonly known as five-twenties outstanding and uncalled, and, whenever all such five-twenty bonds shall have been redeemed, the provisions of this section and all existing provisions of law authorizing the refunding of the national debt shall apply to any bonds of the United States bearing interest at five per centum per annum or a higher rate, which may be redeemable.   In any exchange made under the provisions of this section interest may be allowed, on the bonds redeemed, for a period of three months.

[Approved, January 25, 1879.   20 Statutes at Large, 205.]

XXXVII. . . . **February, 1879.** — *An Act to authorize the issue of certificates of deposit in aid of the refunding of the public debt.*

Be it enacted, . . . That the Secretary of the Treasury is hereby authorized and directed to issue, in exchange for lawful money of the United States that may be presented for such exchange, certificates of deposit, of the denomination of ten dollars, bearing interest at the rate of four per centum per annum, and convertible at any time, with accrued interest into the four per centum bonds described in the refunding act; and the money so received shall be applied only to the payment of the bonds bearing interest at a rate of not less than five per centum in the mode prescribed by said act, and he is authorized to prescribe suitable rules and regulations in conformity with this act.

[Approved, February 26, 1879.   20 Statutes at Large, 321.]

XXXVIII. . . . **February, 1880.** — *An Act authorizing the conversion of national gold banks.*

Be it enacted, . . . That any national gold bank organized under the provisions of the laws of the United States, may, in the manner and subject to the provisions prescribed by section fifty-one hundred and fifty-four of the Revised Statutes of the United States, for the conversion of banks incorporated under the laws of any State. cease to be a gold bank, and become such an association as is authorized, by section fifty-one hundred and thirty-three, for carrying on the business of banking, and shall have the same powers and privileges, and shall be subject to the same duties, responsibilities, and rules, in all respects, as are by law prescribed for such associations : *Provided,* That all certificates of organization which shall be issued under this act shall bear the date of the original organization of each bank respectively as a gold bank.

[Approved, February 14, 1880.   21 Statutes at Large, 66.]

[The provisions of sections 5133 and 5154 of the Revised Statutes are in substance those of section 5 of the Act of June 3, 1864, on page 23, and section 44 of the same Act, on page 32.]

XXXIX. . . . **March, 1881.** — *An Act making appropriations for sundry civil expenses of the Government for the fiscal year ending June thirtieth, eighteen hundred and eighty-two, and for other purposes.*

SEC. 2. That the Secretary of the Treasury may at any time apply the surplus money in the Treasury not otherwise appropriated, or so much thereof as he may consider proper, to the purchase or redemption of United States bonds: *Provided*, That the bonds so purchased or redeemed shall constitute no part of the sinking-fund, but shall be cancelled.

[Approved, March 3, 1881. 21 Statutes at Large, 457.]

XL. . . . **July, 1882.** — *An Act to enable national-banking associations to extend their corporate existence, and for other purposes.*

Be it enacted, . . . That any national banking association organized under the acts of February twenty-fifth, eighteen hundred and sixty-three, June third, eighteen hundred and sixty-four, and February fourteenth, eighteen hundred and eighty, or under sections fifty-one hundred and thirty-three, fifty-one hundred and thirty-four, fifty-one hundred and thirty-five, fifty-one hundred and thirty-six, and fifty-one hundred and fifty-four of the Revised Statutes of the United States, may, at any time within the two years next previous to the date of the expiration of its corporate existence under present law, and with the approval of the Comptroller of the Currency, to be granted as hereinafter provided, extend its period of succession by amending its articles of association for a term of not more than twenty years from the expiration of the period of succession named in said articles of association, and shall have succession for such extended period, unless sooner dissolved by the act of shareholders owning two thirds of its stock, or unless its franchise becomes forfeited by some violation of law, or unless hereafter modified or repealed.

[The sections 5133-5136 and 5154 of the Revised Statutes contain in substance the provisions of sections 5, 6, 8, and 44 of the Act of June 3, 1864; see pages 23 and 32.]

[Sections 2, 3, and 4 provide that the amended articles of association must receive the written consent of shareholders owning not less than two thirds of the capital stock, and shall not be valid until the Comptroller shall have certified his approval, after making a special examination of the association to determine its condition; and that any association so extending the period of its succession "shall continue to be in all respects the identical association it was before the extension of its period of succession."

Section 5 provides that any shareholder not assenting to the amended articles shall be entitled to receive the appraised value of his shares, and that his shares shall then be sold at public sale.]

SEC. 6. That the circulating notes of any association so extending the period of its succession which shall have been issued to it prior to such extension shall be redeemed at the Treasury of the United States, as provided in section three of the act of June twentieth, eighteen hundred and seventy-four, entitled "An act fixing the amount of United States notes, providing for redistribution of national-bank currency, and for other purposes," and such notes when redeemed shall be forwarded to the Comptroller of the Currency, and destroyed as now provided by law; and at the end of three years from the date of the extension of the corporate existence of each bank the association so extended shall deposit lawful money with the Treasurer of the United States sufficient to redeem the remainder of the circulation which was outstanding at the date of its extension, as provided in sections fifty-two hundred and twenty-two, fifty-two hundred and twenty-four, and fifty-two hundred and twenty-five of the Revised Statutes; and any gain that may arise from the failure to present such circulating notes for redemption shall inure to the benefit of the United States; and from time to time, as such notes are redeemed or lawful money deposited therefor as provided herein, new circulating notes shall be issued as provided by this act, bearing such devices, to be approved by the Secretary of the Treasury, as shall make them readily distinguishable from the circulating notes heretofore issued: *Provided however,* That each banking association which shall obtain the benefit of this act shall reimburse to the Treasury the cost of preparing the plate or plates for such new circulating notes as shall be issued to it.

[Sections 5222, 5224, and 5225 of the Revised Statutes contain in substance the provisions of sections 42 and 43 of the Act of June 3, 1864, on page 32.]

[Section 7 provides that any bank which does not avail itself of the provisions of this act shall be wound up as if the shareholders had voted to go into liquidation, that it shall within six months deposit with the Treasurer of the United States lawful money sufficient to redeem all its outstanding circulating notes, and shall thereupon be discharged from all liability therefor, and that the bonds deposited to secure the same shall then be re-assigned to it.]

Sec. 8. That national banks now organized or hereafter organized, having a capital of one hundred and fifty thousand dollars, or less, shall not be required to keep on deposit, or deposit with the Treasurer of the United States, United States bonds in excess of one fourth of their capital stock as security for their circulating notes; but such banks shall keep on deposit, or deposit with the Treasurer of the United States, the amount of bonds as herein required. And such of those banks having on deposit bonds in excess of that amount are authorized to reduce their circulation by the deposit of lawful money as provided by law; *provided*, That the amount of such circulating notes shall not in any case exceed ninety.per centum of the par value of the bonds deposited as herein provided. . . .

Sec. 9. That any national banking association now organized, or hereafter organized, desiring to withdraw its circulating notes, upon a deposit of lawful money with the Treasurer of the United States, as provided in section four of the act of June twentieth, eighteen hundred and seventy-four, entitled "An act fixing the amount of United States notes, providing for a redistribution of national-bank currency, and for other purposes," or as provided in this act, is authorized to deposit lawful money and withdraw a proportionate amount of the bonds held as security for its circulating notes in the order of such deposits; and no national bank which makes any deposit of lawful money in order to withdraw its circulating notes shall be entitled to receive

any increase of its circulation for the period of six months from the time it made such deposit of lawful money for the purpose aforesaid: *Provided*, That not more than three millions of dollars of lawful money shall be deposited during any calendar month for this purpose: *And provided further*, That the provisions of this section shall not apply to bonds called for redemption by the Secretary of the Treasury, nor to the withdrawal of circulating notes in consequence thereof.

SEC. 10. That upon a deposit of bonds as described by sections fifty-one hundred and fifty-nine and fifty-one hundred and sixty, except as modified by section four of an act entitled "An act fixing the amount of United States notes, providing for a redistribution of the national-bank currency, and for other purposes," approved June twentieth, eighteen hundred and seventy-four, and as modified by section eight, of this act, the association making the same shall be entitled to receive from the Comptroller of the Currency circulating notes of different denominations, in blank, registered and countersigned as provided by law, equal in amount to ninety per centum of the current market value, not exceeding par, of the United States bonds so transferred and delivered, and at no time shall the total amount of such notes issued to any such association exceed ninety per centum of the amount at such time actually paid in of its capital stock; and the provisions of sections fifty-one hundred and seventy-one and fifty-one hundred and seventy-six of the Revised Statutes are hereby repealed.

[Sections 5159 and 5160 of the Revised Statutes correspond to section 16 of the Bank Act of 1864 on page 24; and sections 5171 and 5176 state the limit of circulating notes to be allowed to each bank, as given on pages 43 and 47.]

SEC. 11. That the Secretary of the Treasury is hereby authorized to receive at the Treasury any bonds of the United States bearing three and a half per centum interest, and to issue in exchange therefor an equal amount of registered bonds of the United States of the denominations of fifty, one hundred, five hundred, one thousand, and ten thousand dollars, of such form as he may prescribe, bearing interest at the rate of three per centum per annum, payable quarterly at the Treasury of the United States. Such bonds shall be exempt from all taxation by or under State authority, and be payable at the pleasure of the United States: *Provided*, That the bonds herein authorized shall not be called in and paid so long as any bonds of the United States heretofore issued bearing a higher rate of interest than three per centum, and which shall be redeemable at the pleasure of the United States, shall be outstanding and uncalled. The last of the said bonds originally issued under this act, and their substitutes, shall be first called in, and this order of payment shall be followed until all shall have been paid.

Sec. 12. That the Secretary of the Treasury is authorized and directed to receive deposits of gold coin with the Treasurer or assistant treasurers of the United States, in sums not less than twenty dollars, and to issue certificates therefor in denominations of not less than twenty dollars each, corresponding with the denominations of United States notes. The coin deposited for or representing, the certificates of deposits shall be retained in the Treasury for the payment of the same on demand. Said certificates shall be receivable for customs, taxes, and all public dues, and when so received may be reissued; and such certificates, as also silver certificates, when held by any national banking association, shall be counted as part of its lawful reserve; and no national banking association shall be a member of any clearing-house in which such certificates shall not be receivable in the settlement of clearing-house balances: *Provided*, That the Secretary of the Treasury shall suspend the issue of such gold certificates whenever the amount of gold coin and gold bullion in the Treasury, reserved for the redemption of United States notes falls below one hundred millions of dollars; and the provisions of section fifty-two hundred and seven of the Revised Statutes shall be applicable to the certificates herein authorized and directed to be issued.

Sec. 14. That Congress may at any time amend, alter, or repeal this act and the acts of which this is amendatory.

[Approved, July 12, 1882. 22 Statutes at Large, 162.]

[Section 5207 of the Revised Statutes is the Act of February 19, 1869, on page 45.]

APPENDIX,

CONTAINING LAWS RELATING TO COINAGE.

APPENDIX,

CONTAINING LAWS RELATING TO COINAGE.

I. ... April, 1792. — *An Act establishing a Mint, and regulating the Coins of the United States.*

SEC. 9. *And be it further enacted,* That there shall be from time to time struck and coined at the said mint, coins of gold, silver, and copper, of the following denominations, values and descriptions, viz. EAGLES — each to be of the value of ten dollars or units, and to contain two hundred and forty-seven grains and four-eighths of a grain of pure, or two hundred and seventy grains of standard gold.

[Half eagles and quarter eagles of corresponding weights and fineness.]

DOLLARS OR UNITS — Each to be of the value of a Spanish milled dollar as the same is now current, and to contain three hundred and seventy-one grains and four-sixteenth parts of a grain of pure, or four hundred and sixteen grains of standard silver.

[Half dollars, quarter dollars, dimes, and half dimes of corresponding weights and fineness.]

SEC. 11. *And be it further enacted,* That the proportional value of gold to silver in all coins which shall by law be current as money within the United States, shall be as fifteen to one, according to quantity in weight, of pure gold or pure silver; that is to say, every fifteen pounds weight of pure silver shall be of equal value in all payments, with one pound weight of pure gold, and so in proportion as to any greater or less quantities of the respective metals.

SEC. 14. *And be it further enacted,* That it shall be lawful for any person or persons to bring to the said mint gold and silver bullion, in order to their being coined; and that the bullion so brought shall be there assayed and coined as speedily as may be after the receipt thereof, and that free of expense to the person or persons by whom the same shall have been brought. And as soon as the said bullion shall have been coined, the person or persons by whom the same shall have been delivered, shall upon demand receive in lieu thereof coins of the same species of bullion which shall have been so delivered, weight for weight, of the pure gold or pure silver therein contained: *Provided nevertheless,* That it shall be at the mutual option of the party or parties bringing such bullion, and of the director of the said mint, to make an immediate exchange of coins for standard bullion, with a deduction of one-half per cent. from the weight of pure gold, or pure silver contained in the said bullion, as an indemnification to the mint for the time which will necessarily be required for coining the said bullion, and for the advance which shall have been so made in coins.

SEC. 16. *And be it further enacted,* That all the gold and silver coins which shall have been struck at, and issued from the said mint, shall be a lawful tender in all payments whatsoever, those of full weight according to the respective values herein before declared, and those of less than full weight at values proportional to their respective weights.

[Approved, April 2, 1792. 1 Statutes at Large, 246.]

II. ... June, 1834. — *An Act concerning the gold coins of the United States, and for other purposes.*

Be it enacted, . . . That the gold coins of the United States shall contain the following quantities of metal, that is to say: each eagle shall contain two hundred and thirty-two grains of pure gold, and two hundred and fifty-eight grains of standard gold; each half eagle one hundred and sixteen grains of pure gold, and one hundred and twenty-nine grains of standard gold;

each quarter eagle shall contain fifty-eight grains of pure gold, and sixty-four and a half grains of standard gold; every such eagle shall be of the value of ten dollars; every such half eagle shall be of the value of five dollars; and every such quarter eagle shall be of the value of two dollars and fifty cents; and the said gold coins shall be receivable in all payments, when of full weight, according to their respective values; and when of less than full weight, at less values, proportioned to their respective actual weights.

SEC. 2. *And be it further enacted*, That all standard gold or silver deposited for coinage after the thirty-first of July next, shall be paid for in coin under the direction of the Secretary of the Treasury, within five days from the making of such deposit, deducting from the amount of said deposit of gold and silver one-half of one per centum: *Provided*, That no deduction shall be made unless said advance be required by such depositor within forty days.

SEC. 3. *And be it further enacted*, That all gold coins of the United States, minted anterior to the thirty-first day of July next, shall be receivable in all payments at the rate of ninety-four and eight-tenths of a cent per pennyweight.

[Approved, June 28, 1834.   4 Statutes at Large, 699.]

III.... January, 1837. — *An Act supplementary to the act entitled " An act establishing a mint, and regulating the coins of the United States."*

SEC. 8. *And be it further enacted*, That the standard for both gold and silver coins of the United States shall hereafter be such, that of one thousand parts by weight, nine hundred shall be of pure metal, and one hundred of alloy; and the alloy of the silver coins shall be of copper; and the alloy of the gold coins shall be of copper and silver, provided that the silver do not exceed one-half of the whole alloy.

SEC. 9. *And be it further enacted*, That of the silver coins, the dollar shall be of the weight of four hundred and twelve and one-half grains; the half dollar of the weight of two hundred and six and one-fourth grains; the quarter dollar of the

weight of one hundred and three and one-eighth grains; the
dime, or tenth part of a dollar, of the weight of forty-one and
a quarter grains; and the half dime, or twentieth part of a dollar, of the weight of twenty grains, and five-eighths of a grain.
And that dollars, half dollars, and quarter dollars, dimes, and
half dimes, shall be legal tenders of payment, according to their
nominal value, for any sums whatever.

SEC. 10. *And be it further enacted,* That of the gold coins,
the weight of the eagle shall be two hundred and fifty-eight
grains; that of the half eagle one hundred and twenty-nine
grains; and that of the quarter eagle sixty-four and one-half
grains. And that for all sums whatever, the eagle shall be a
legal tender of payment for ten dollars; the half eagle for five
dollars; and the quarter eagle for two and a half dollars.

SEC. 11. *And be it further enacted,* That the silver coins
heretofore issued at the mint of the United States, and the gold
coins issued since the thirty-first day of July, one thousand eight
hundred and thirty-four, shall continue to be legal tenders of
payment for their nominal values, on the same terms as if they
were of the coinage provided for by this act.

[Approved, January 18, 1837. 5 Statutes at Large, 136.]

IV. . . . March, 1849. — *An Act to authorize the Coinage of Gold
Dollars and Double Eagles.*

[This act authorizes the coinage of gold dollars and double eagles,
"conformably in all respects to the standard for gold coins now established by law," and to be a legal tender in payment for all sums.]

[Approved, March 3, 1849. 9 Statutes at Large, 397.]

V. . . . February, 1853. — *An Act amendatory of Existing Laws
relative to the Half Dollar, Quarter Dollar, Dime, and Half
Dime.*

Be it enacted, . . . That from and after the first day of June,
eighteen hundred and fifty-three, the weight of the half dollar or
piece of fifty cents shall be one hundred and ninety-two grains,
and the quarter dollar, dime, and half dime, shall be, respectively, one-half, one-fifth, and one-tenth of the weight of said
half dollar.

SEC. 2. *And be it further enacted,* That the silver coins issued in conformity with the above section, shall be legal tenders in payment of debts for all sums not exceeding five dollars.

SEC. 3. *And be it further enacted,* That in order to procure bullion for the requisite coinage of the subdivisions of the dollar authorized by this act, the Treasurer of the Mint shall, with the approval of the Director, purchase such bullion with the bullion fund of the mint. . . .

SEC. 4. *And be it further enacted,* That such coins shall be paid out at the mint, in exchange for gold coins at par, in sums not less than one hundred dollars ; and it shall be lawful, also, to transmit parcels of the same from time to time to the assistant treasurers, depositaries, and other officers of the United States, under general regulations, proposed by the Director of the Mint, and approved by the Secretary of the Treasury : *Provided, however,* That the amount coined into quarter dollars, dimes, and half dimes, shall be regulated by the Secretary of the Treasury.

SEC. 5. *And be it further enacted,* That no deposits for coinage into the half dollar, quarter dollar, dime, and half dime, shall hereafter be received, other than those made by the Treasurer of the Mint, as herein authorized, and upon account of the United States.

[Section 6 provides that when gold or silver is deposited for coinage, there shall be a charge to the depositor, in addition to the charge for refining or parting the metals, of one half of one per centum, this provision not applying to silver coined into the subdivisions of the dollar.]

SEC. 7. *And be it further enacted,* That from time to time there shall be struck and coined at the Mint of the United States, and the branches thereof, conformably in all respects to law, and conformably in all respects to the standard of gold coins now established by law, a coin of gold of the value of three dollars, or units. . . .

[Approved, February 21, 1853. 10 Statutes at Large, 160.]

VI . . . February, 1873. — *An Act revising and amending the Laws relative to the Mints, Assay-offices, and Coinage of the United States.*

SEC. 14. That the gold coins of the United States shall be a one-dollar piece, which, at the standard weight of twenty-five and eight-tenths grains, shall be the unit of value; a quarter-eagle, or two-and-a-half dollar piece; a three-dollar piece; a half-eagle, or five-dollar piece; an eagle or ten-dollar piece; and a double eagle, or twenty-dollar piece. And the standard weight of the gold dollar shall be twenty-five and eight-tenths grains; of the quarter-eagle, or two-and-a-half dollar piece, sixty-four and a half grains; of the three-dollar piece, seventy-seven and four-tenths grains; of the half-eagle, or five-dollar piece, one hundred and twenty-nine grains; of the eagle, or ten-dollar piece, two hundred and fifty-eight grains; of the double eagle, or twenty-dollar piece, five hundred and sixteen grains; which coins shall be a legal tender in all payments at their nominal value when not below the standard weight and limit of tolerance provided in this act for the single piece, and, when reduced in weight, below said standard and tolerance, shall be a legal tender at valuation in proportion to their actual weight; and any gold coin of the United States, if reduced in weight by natural abrasion not more than one-half of one per centum below the standard weight prescribed by law, after a circulation of twenty years, as shown by its date of coinage, and at a ratable proportion for any period less than twenty years, shall be received at their nominal value by the United States treasury and its offices. . . .

Sec. 15. That the silver coins of the United States shall be a trade-dollar, a half-dollar, or fifty cent piece, a quarter-dollar, or twenty-five cent piece, a dime or ten-cent piece; and the weight of the trade-dollar shall be four hundred and twenty grains troy; the weight of the half-dollar shall be twelve grams (grammes) and one-half of a gram, (gramme); the quarter-dollar and the dime shall be respectively, one-half and one-fifth of the weight of said half-dollar; and said coins shall be a legal tender at their nominal value for any amount not exceeding five dollars in any one payment.

Sec. 17. That no coins, either of gold, silver, or minor coinage, shall hereafter be issued from the mint other than those of the denominations, standards, and weights herein set forth.

Sec. 25. That the charge for converting standard gold bullion into coin shall be one-fifth of one per centum; and the charges for converting standard silver into trade-dollars, for melting and

refining when bullion is below standard, for toughening when metals are contained in it which render it unfit for coinage, for copper used for alloy when the bullion is above standard, for separating the gold and silver when these metals exist together in the bullion, and for the preparation of bars, shall be fixed, from time to time, by the director, with the concurrence of the Secretary of the Treasury, so as to equal but not exceed, in their judgment, the actual average cost to each mint and assay-office of the material, labor, wastage, and use of machinery employed in each of the cases aforementioned.

[Approved, February 12, 1873.   17 Statutes at Large, 424.]

NOTE. — By an Act approved March 3, 1875, the coinage of a twenty cent piece, in conformity with the provisions made as to other subsidiary silver coins, was authorized.   See 18 Statutes at Large, part 3, 478

This act was repealed May 2, 1878.

VII. . . . June, 1874. — *Revised Statutes of the United States ; Title* xxxix., *Legal Tender.*

SEC. 3584. No foreign gold or silver coins shall be a legal tender in payment of debts.

SEC. 3585. The gold coins of the United States shall be a legal tender in all payments at their nominal value when not below the standard weight and limit of tolerance provided by law for the single piece, and, when reduced in weight below such standard and tolerance, shall be a legal tender at valuation in proportion to their actual weight.

SEC. 3586. The silver coins of the United States shall be a legal tender at their nominal value for any amount not exceeding five dollars in any one payment.

SEC. 3587. The minor coins of the United States shall be a legal tender, at their nominal value for any amount not exceeding twenty-five cents in any one payment.

[Sections 3588, 3589, 3590, contain the provisions to be found in previous acts, making United States notes, demand notes, and Treasury notes, respectively, legal tender.]

[Approved, June 22, 1874.   Revised Statutes, 712.]

VIII. . . . January, 1875. — *An Act to provide for the resumption of specie payments.*

[For sections 1 and 2 of this act, providing for the coinage of small silver coins and their issue in redemption of fractional currency, and for the discontinuance of the charge made for coining gold bullion, see *ante*, p. 57.]

[Approved, January 14, 1875. 18 Statutes at Large, part 3, 296.]

IX. . . . July, 1876. — *Joint Resolution for the Issue of silver coin.*

Resolved, . . . That the Secretary of the Treasury, under such limits and regulations as will best secure a just and fair distribution of the same through the country, may issue the silver coin at any time in the Treasury to an amount not exceeding ten million dollars, in exchange for an equal amount of legal-tender notes; and the notes so received in exchange shall be kept as a special fund separate and apart from all other money in the Treasury, and be reissued only upon the retirement and destruction of a like sum of fractional currency received at the Treasury in payment of dues to the United States; and said fractional currency, when so substituted, shall be destroyed and held as part of the sinking fund, as provided in the act approved April seventeen, eighteen hundred and seventy-six.

SEC. 2. That the trade dollar shall not hereafter be a legal tender, and the Secretary of the Treasury is hereby authorized to limit from time to time, the coinage thereof to such an amount as he may deem sufficient to meet the export demand for the same.

SEC. 3. That in addition to the amount of subsidiary silver coin authorized by law to be issued in redemption of the fractional currency it shall be lawful to manufacture at the several mints, and issue through the Treasury and its several offices, such coin, to an amount, that, including the amount of subsidiary silver coin and of fractional currency outstanding, shall, in the aggregate, not exceed, at any time, fifty million dollars.

[Section 4 authorizes the Secretary of the Treasury to purchase bullion for the purposes of this resolution, and requires any gain arising from the coinage thereof to be paid into the Treasury.]

[Approved, July 22, 1876. 19 Statutes at Large, 215.]

X. . . . February, 1878. — *An Act to authorize the coinage of the standard silver dollar, and to restore its legal-tender character.*

Be it enacted, . . . That there shall be coined, at the several mints of the United States, silver dollars of the weight of four hundred and twelve and a half grains Troy of standard silver, as provided in the act of January eighteenth, eighteen hundred thirty-seven, on which shall be the devices and superscriptions provided by said act ; which coins together with all silver dollars heretofore coined by the United States, of like weight and fineness, shall be a legal tender, at their nominal value, for all debts and dues public and private, except where otherwise expressly stipulated in the contract. And the Secretary of the Treasury is authorized and directed to purchase, from time to time, silver bullion, at the market price thereof, not less than two million dollars worth per month, nor more than four million dollars worth per month, and cause the same to be coined monthly, as fast as so purchased, into such dollars ; and a sum sufficient to carry out the foregoing provision of this act is hereby appropriated out of any money in the Treasury not otherwise appropriated. And any gain or seigniorage arising from this coinage shall be accounted for and paid into the Treasury, as provided under existing laws relative to the subsidiary coinage : *Provided,* That the amount of money at any one time invested in such silver bullion, exclusive of such resulting coin, shall not exceed five million dollars : *And provided further,* That nothing in this act shall be construed to authorize the payment in silver of certificates of deposit issued under the provisions of section two hundred and fifty-four of the Revised Statutes.

[The provisions of section 254 of the Revised Statutes are contained in section 5 of the act of March 3, 1863, on page 21.]

Sec. 2. That immediately after the passage of this act, the President shall invite the governments of the countries composing the Latin Union, so called, and of such other European nations as he may deem advisable, to join the United States in a conference to adopt a common ratio between gold and silver,

for the purpose of establishing, internationally, the use of bime-
tallic money, and securing fixity of relative value between those
metals; such conference to be held at such place, in Europe or
in the United States, at such time within six months, as may be
mutually agreed upon by the executives of the governments
joining in the same, whenever the governments so invited, or
any three of them, shall have signified their willingness to unite
in the same.

The President shall, by and with the advice and consent of
the Senate, appoint three commissioners, who shall attend such
conference on behalf of the United States, and shall report the
doings thereof to the President, who shall transmit the same to
Congress.

Said commissioners shall each receive the sum of two thousand
five hundred dollars and their reasonable expenses, to be approved
by the Secretary of State; and the amount necessary to pay such
compensation and expenses is hereby appropriated out of any
money in the Treasury not otherwise appropriated.

SEC. 3. That any holder of the coin authorized by this act
may deposit the same with the Treasurer or any assistant
treasurer of the United States, in sums not less than ten dollars, and receive therefor certificates of not less than ten dollars
each, corresponding with the denominations of the United States
notes. The coin deposited for or representing the certificates
shall be retained in the Treasury for the payment of the same
on demand. Said certificates shall be receivable for customs,
taxes, and all public dues, and, when so received, may be reissued.

SEC. 4. All acts and parts of acts inconsistent with the provisions of this act are hereby repealed.

NOTE. — The above act having been returned by the President of the
United States, with his objections, to the House of Representatives, February 28, 1878, was passed by both Houses, and became a law on the
same day.

[20 Statutes at Large, 25.]

XI . . . May, 1882. — *An Act to authorize the receipt of United States gold coin in exchange for gold bars.*

Be it enacted, . . . That the superintendents of the coinage mints, and of the United States assay-office at New York, are hereby authorized to receive United States gold coin from any holder thereof in sums not less than five thousand dollars, and to pay and deliver in exchange therefor gold bars in value equalling such coin so received.

[Approved, May 26, 1882.   22 Statutes at Large, 97.]

www.ingramcontent.com/pod-product-compliance
Lightning Source LLC
Chambersburg PA
CBHW030554270326
41927CB00007B/915